STEP INTO THE

AZTEC & MAYA

WORLDS

Fiona Macdonald

Consultant: Clara Bezanilla, The Museum of Mankind

HERMES
HOUSE

This edition is published
by Hermes House

Hermes House is an imprint of
Anness Publishing Ltd
Hermes House, 88–89
Blackfriars Road
London SE1 8HA
tel. 020 7401 2077; fax 020 7633 9499
www.hermeshouse.com;
www.annesspublishing.com

If you like the images in this book and would like to
investigate using them for publishing, promotions or
advertising, please visit our website
www.practicalpictures.com for more information.

A CIP catalogue record for this book is available from
the British Library.

Publisher: Joanna Lorenz
Managing Editor, Children's Books: Sue Grabham
Senior Editor: Nicole Pearson
Editor: Nicola Baxter
Proofreader: Felicity Forster
Designer: Caroline Reeves
Illustration: Rob Ashby, Julian Baker, Stuart Carter
and Stephen Gyapay
Special Photography: John Freeman
Stylist: Konika Shankar
Production Controller: Ann Childers

Anness Publishing would like to thank the following
children for modelling for this book: Anthony
Bainbridge, Ricky Garrett, Sasha Haworth, Alex
Lindblom-Smith, Lucy Nightingale, Ifi Obi, Mai-Anh
Peterson, Charlie Ray, Joseph Williams.

PICTURE CREDITS

b=bottom, t=top, c=centre, l=left, r=right

The Bridgeman Art Library: 9tl, 45bl; GDR Barnett Images:
20tl; 21bl, 42bl; The British Museum: front cover; The
Bodleian Library: 13cl, 14b, 15br, 17c; Bruce Coleman: 27c;
Dagli Orti 59tl; James Davis: 1, 8br, 18tl, 39bl, 50c, 52tl,
59br; C M Dixon: 10tl, 14tl, 16r, 27bl; E T Archive: 9br,
10br, 11bl, 11tr, 13tl, 15bl, 21tr, 22tl, 23br, 24tl, 24bl, 25br,
26tl, 27tr, 28c, 30, 31, 32b, 33, 35tl, 36bl, 39r, 41tl, 41tr,
41bl, 42tl, 47tl, 51l, 51tr, 52c, 53c, 54, 55, 56cr, 56tl, 58t,
60br ; Mary Evans Picture Library: 22br, 39tl, 60tl; Werner
Forman Archive: 4tl, 15tr, 16tl, 28tl, 36tl, 55tl; Michael
Holford: 5c, 11br, 12br, 34tl, 43tr, 50tl, 51r, 61; Hutchison:
37c; NHPA: 27c; Planet Earth Pictures: 25c; South American
Photo Library 4br, 5tl, 8tl, 9tl, 12tl, 13tr, 17tl, 18tr, 19tr,
20b, 22bl, 23bl, 24br, 26bl, 29tr, 30bl, 33br, 35bl, 37, 43br,
44tl, 46c, 48c, 53b, 57tl, 57c, 58b, 61; Visual Arts Library:
10br, 19t, 19b, 27tl, 29tc, 29tl, 32tl, 33tl, 38cr, 40c, 40tl,
43bl, 45, 46tl, 47tr, 55tl, 56tr, 56cl, 59tr, 60bl; Zefa: 43tr.

CONTENTS

Great Civilizations

THE AZTECS LIVED IN MESOAMERICA — the region where North and South America meet. It includes the countries of Mexico, Guatemala, Honduras, El Salvador and Belize. During the past 3,000 years, Mesoamerica has been home to many great civilizations, including the Olmecs, the Maya, the Toltecs and the Aztecs. The Aztecs were the last of these to arrive, coming from the north in around AD1200. In about 1420 they began to conquer a mighty empire. But in 1521 they were themselves conquered by Spanish soldiers, who came to America in search of gold. Over the next hundred years, the rest of Mesoamerica also fell to the Spaniards.

Even so, the descendants of these cultures still live in the area today. Many ancient Mesoamerican words, customs and beliefs survive, as do beautiful hand-painted books, mysterious ruins and amazing treasures.

OLMEC POWER
This giant stone head was carved by the Olmecs, the earliest of many great civilizations that flourished in Mesoamerica. Like the Maya and Aztecs, the Olmecs were skilled stone workers and built great cities.

UNCOVERING THE PAST
This temple is in Belize. Remains of such great buildings give archaeologists important clues about the people who built them.

TIMELINE 5000BC–AD800

Many civilizations were powerful in Mesoamerica at different times. The Maya were most successful between AD600–900. The Aztecs were at the height of their power from AD1428–AD1520.

5000BC The Maya settle along the Pacific and Caribbean coasts of Mesoamerica.

2000BC People begin to farm in Guatemala, Belize and south-east Mexico.

Olmec figure

2000BC The beginning of the period known as the Preclassic era.

1200BC Olmec people are powerful in Mesoamerica. They remain an important power until 400BC.

1000BC Maya craftworkers begin to copy Olmec pottery and jade carvings.

900BC Maya farmers design and use irrigation systems.

600BC The Zapotec civilization begins to flourish at Monte Alban.

Maya codex

300BC The Maya population starts to grow rapidly. Cities are built.

292BC The first-known Maya writing is produced.

150BC–AD500 The people living in the city of Teotihuacan grow powerful.

AD250 The beginning of the greatest period of Maya power, known as the Classic Maya era. This lasts until AD900.

mask from Teotihuacan

5000BC   2000BC   300BC   AD500

THE GREAT TEMPLE

The Maya built this pyramid at Chichen-Itza in south-eastern Mexico, around AD1000. Historians believe that the Putun people may also have established themselves at Chichen-Itza. The pyramid was designed so that twice a year the Sun casts a snake-shaped shadow down the steps. Buildings like this tell us about the religious beliefs of the Maya and also show what skilful builders they were. Maya and Aztec stone masons worked without the help of metal tools.

THE FACE OF A GOD

This mask represents the god Tezcatlipoca. It is made of pieces of semi-precious stone fixed to a real human skull. Masks like this were worn during religious ceremonies, or displayed in temples as offerings to the gods.

MESSAGES IN CODE

These are Aztec picture-symbols for days, written in a folding book called a codex. Mesoamerican civilizations kept records of important people, places and events in picture-writing.

■ Home of the Mesoamerican civilizations

MESOAMERICA IN THE WORLD

For centuries, Mesoamerica was home to many different civilizations, but there were links between them, especially in farming, technology and religious beliefs. Until around AD1500, these Mesoamerican civilizations had very little contact with the rest of the world.

AD550 This is the time of the Maya's greatest artistic achievements. Fine temples and palaces in cities such as Kabah, Copan, Palenque, Uxmal and Tikal are built. These great regional city-states are ruled by lords who claim to be descended from the gods. This period of Maya success continues until AD900.

temple at Tikal

AD615 The great Maya leader Lord Pacal rules in the city of Palenque.

AD650 The city of Teotihuacan begins to decline. It is looted and burned by unknown invaders around AD700.

AD684 Lord Pacal's rule in Palenque ends. He is buried in a tomb within the Temple of the Inscriptions.

jade death mask of Lord Pacal

Bonampak mural

AD790 Splendid Maya wall-paintings are created in the royal palace in the city of Bonampak.

AD600   AD700   AD800

Between North and South

MESOAMERICA IS A LAND of contrasts. There are high, jagged mountains, harsh deserts and swampy lakes. In the north, volcanoes rumble. In the south, dense, steamy forests have constant rain for half the year. These features made travelling around difficult, and also restricted contact between the regions.

Mesoamerica was never ruled as a single, united country. For centuries it was divided into separate states, each based on a city that ruled the surrounding countryside. Different groups of people and their cities became rich and strong in turn, before their civilizations weakened and faded away.

Historians divide the Mesoamerican past into three main periods. In Preclassic times (2000BC–AD250), the Olmecs were most powerful. The Classic era (AD250–900) saw the rise of the Maya and the people living in the city of Teotihuacan. During the Postclassic era (AD900–1500), the Toltecs, followed by the Aztecs, controlled the strongest states.

Each civilization had its own language, laws, traditions and skills, but there were also many links between the separate states. They all built big cities and organized long-distance trade. They all practised human sacrifice and worshipped the same family of gods. And, unlike all other ancient American people, they all measured time using their own holy calendar of 260 days.

Sierra Madre Occidental

MEXICO

N

TIMELINE AD800–AD1400

AD800 The Maya palace-city of Palenque begins to decline.

AD856 The Toltecs of northern Mexico begin to create the city-state of Tula.

Palenque

AD900 Maya power begins to collapse. Many Maya cities, temples and palaces are deserted and overgrown by the rainforest. This is the beginning of the period known as the Postclassic era. The era lasts until AD1500.

AD950 The city of Tula becomes the centre of fast-growing Toltec power.

AD986 According to legend, the Toltec god-king Quetzalcoatl leaves north Mexico for the Maya lands of Yucatan.

Toltec warrior

AD1000 The Maya city of Chichen-Itza becomes powerful. Historians believe that the Maya may have been helped by Putun warriors from the Gulf coast of Mexico.

AD1000 Toltec merchants do business along long-distance trade routes around the coast. They are helped by Maya craftworkers. Long-distance trade has already been taking place in Mesoamerica for hundreds of years.

AD1011–1063 The Mixtecs are ruled by the leader Eight Deer, in the area of Oaxaca. The Mixtecs are master goldsmiths.

AD800　　　　　　　　　AD900　　　　　　　　　AD1000　　　　　　　　　AD1100

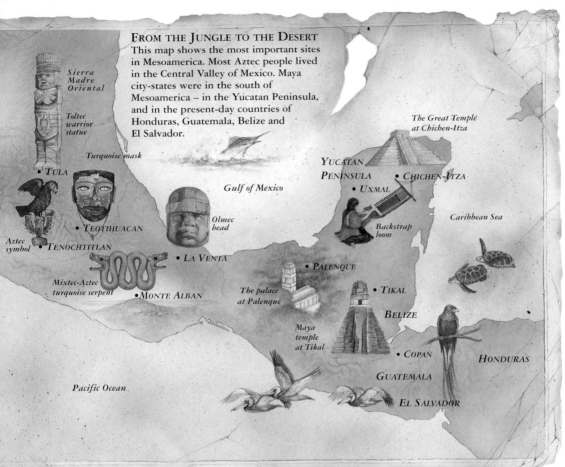

FROM THE JUNGLE TO THE DESERT

This map shows the most important sites in Mesoamerica. Most Aztec people lived in the Central Valley of Mexico. Maya city-states were in the south of Mesoamerica – in the Yucatan Peninsula, and in the present-day countries of Honduras, Guatemala, Belize and El Salvador.

Sierra Madre Oriental

Toltec warrior statue

Turquoise mask

TULA

Aztec symbol

TEOTIHUACAN

TENOCHTITLAN

Mixtec-Aztec turquoise serpent

MONTE ALBAN

Pacific Ocean

Gulf of Mexico

Olmec head

LA VENTA

The Great Temple at Chichen-Itza

YUCATAN PENINSULA

CHICHEN-ITZA

UXMAL

Backstrap loom

Caribbean Sea

PALENQUE

The palace at Palenque

TIKAL

BELIZE

Maya temple at Tikal

COPAN

HONDURAS

GUATEMALA

EL SALVADOR

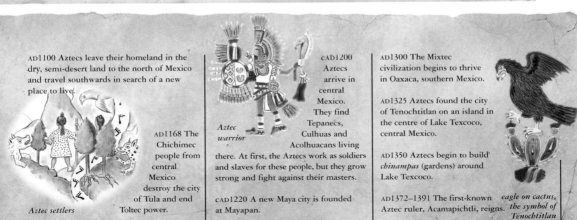

AD1100 Aztecs leave their homeland in the dry, semi-desert land to the north of Mexico and travel southwards in search of a new place to live.

Aztec settlers

AD1168 The Chichimec people from central Mexico destroy the city of Tula and end Toltec power.

Aztec warrior

cAD1200 Aztecs arrive in central Mexico. They find Tepanecs, Culhuas and Acolhuacans living there. At first, the Aztecs work as soldiers and slaves for these people, but they grow strong and fight against their masters.

cAD1220 A new Maya city is founded at Mayapan.

AD1300 The Mixtec civilization begins to thrive in Oaxaca, southern Mexico.

AD1325 Aztecs found the city of Tenochtitlan on an island in the centre of Lake Texcoco, central Mexico.

AD1350 Aztecs begin to build *chinampas* (gardens) around Lake Texcoco.

AD1372–1391 The first-known Aztec ruler, Acamapichtli, reigns.

eagle on cactus, the symbol of Tenochtitlan

AD1200   AD1300   AD1400

Famous People

FAME IN Maya and Aztec times usually came with power. We know the names of powerful Aztec and Maya rulers, and sometimes of their wives. However, very few ordinary people's names have been discovered.

Rulers' names were written in a codex or carved on a monument to record success in battle or other great achievements. Scribes also compiled family histories, in which rulers often claimed to be descended from gods. This gave them extra religious power. Aztec and Maya rulers made sure their names lived on by building huge palaces, amazing temples and tombs.

Some of the most famous Mesoamerican rulers lived at a time when their civilization was under threat from outsiders. Explorers from Europe have left us detailed accounts and descriptions of the rulers they met.

ROYAL TOMB
This pyramid-shaped temple was built to house the tomb of Lord Pacal. He ruled the Maya city-state of Palenque from AD615 to 684. Its walls are decorated with scenes from Pacal's life.

MAYA RULER
This statue shows a ruler from the Maya city of Kabah, in Mexico. Most Maya statues were designed as symbols of power, rather than as life-like portraits.

TIMELINE AD1400–AD1600

tribute items collected by the Aztecs

AD1400–AD1425 The Aztec city of Tenochtitlan continues to thrive and grow.

AD1415–1426 The Aztec leader Chimalpopoca reigns.

AD1428 Aztecs defeat the Tepanecs and begin to conquer neighbouring lands and collect tribute from them.

AD1428 Aztecs set up the Triple Alliance. This was an agreement with neighbouring city-states Texcoco and Tlacopan that made them the strongest force in Mexico.

AD1440 Moctezuma Ilhuicamina, the greatest Aztec ruler, begins his reign. He reigns until 1468.

AD1441 The Maya city of Mayapan is destroyed by civil war.

AD1468 Aztec ruler Axayacatl reigns.

AD1473 The Aztecs conquer the rich market-city of Tlatelolco in central Mexico.

market traders in the market-city of Tlatelolco

AD1400   AD1425   AD1450   AD1475

GOLD-SEEKER

Soldier and explorer Hernan Cortes (1485–1547) came from a poor but noble Spanish family. After Columbus' voyages, many Spanish adventurers travelled to Mesoamerica and the Caribbean hoping to make their fortunes. Cortes sailed to Cuba and then, in 1519, went on to explore Mexico. His example inspired many treasure-seekers. One such man, Pizarro, went on to conquer the Incas of Peru.

BETWEEN TWO WORLDS

Malintzin (*far right above*) was from a Mesoamerican state hostile to the Aztecs. She was of vital help to the Spanish conquerors because she spoke the Aztec language and quickly learned Spanish. The Spanish called her Doña Marina.

THE LAST EMPEROR

Aztec emperor Moctezuma II (*above right*) ruled from 1502 to 1520. He was the last emperor to control the Aztec lands. Moctezuma II was a powerful warrior and a good administrator, but he was tormented by gloomy prophecies and visions of disaster. He was captured when Cortes and his soldiers invaded the capital city of Tenochtitlan in 1519. The following year he was stoned in a riot whilst trying to plead with his own people.

AD1481 1486 Aztec ruler Tizoc reigns.

AD1486 Aztec ruler Ahuitzotl begins his reign.

AD1487 The Aztecs' Great Temple in Tenochtitlan is finished. Twenty thousand captives are sacrificed at a special ceremony to consecrate it (make it holy).

AD1492 The European explorer Christopher Columbus sails across the Atlantic Ocean to America.

Columbus lands

AD1502 Columbus sails along the coast of Mesoamerica and meets Maya people.

a comet appears in the sky

AD1502–1520 Moctezuma II reigns. During his reign, a comet appears in the sky. Aztec astronomers fear that this, and other strange signs, mean the end of the world.

AD1519 Hernan Cortes, a Spanish soldier, arrives in Mexico. A year later, Cortes and his soldiers attack Tenochtitlan. Moctezuma II is killed.

AD1521 The Spanish destroy Tenochtitlan.

AD1525 Spain takes control of Aztec lands.

AD1527 Maya lands are invaded by the Spanish.

AD1535 Mexico becomes a Spanish colony.

AD1600 War and European diseases wipe out 10 million Aztecs, leaving fewer than a million, but the Aztec language and many customs live on. By AD1600, between 75% and 90% of Maya people are also dead, but Maya skills, beliefs and traditions survive.

Spanish soldier

AD1500   AD1525   AD1600

The Order of Things

MESOAMERICAN CITY-STATES were ruled by leaders with three separate tasks. They were army commanders, law-makers and priests. Many rulers claimed to be descended from the gods. Rulers were almost always men. Mesoamerican women – especially among the Maya – had important religious duties but rarely took part in law-making or army life.

Maya rulers were called *ahaw* (lord) or *mahk'ina* (great Sun lord), and each city-state had its own royal family. The Aztec leader was called the *tlatoani* (speaker). Originally, he was elected from army commanders by the Aztec people. Later, he was chosen from the family of the previous ruler. He ruled all Aztec lands, helped by a deputy called *cihuacoatl* (snake woman), by nobles and by army commanders. Priests observed the stars, looking for signs about the future, and held religious ceremonies.

Rulers, priests and nobles made up a tiny part of society. Ordinary citizens were called *macehualtin*. Women looked after their families. Men were farmers, fishermen or craftworkers. There were also thousands of slaves, who were criminals, enemy captives or poor people who had given up their freedom in return for food and shelter.

OFFICIAL HELP
This Maya clay figure shows a scribe at work. Well-trained officials, such as this scribe, helped Mesoamerican rulers by keeping careful records. Scribes also painted ceremonial pottery.

HONOUR TO THE KING
Painted pottery vases like this were buried alongside powerful Maya people. They show scenes from legends and royal palace life. Here, a lord presents tribute to the king.

MAYA NOBLEWOMAN
This terracotta figure of a Maya noblewoman dates from between AD600 and 900. She is richly attired and is protecting her face with a parasol. Women did not usually hold official positions of responsibility in Mesoamerican lands. Instead queens and other noblewomen influenced their husbands by offering tactful suggestions and wise advice. Whether she was rich or poor, a woman's main duty was to provide children for her husband and to support him in all aspects of his work.

THE RULING CLASS

A noble is shown getting ready for a ceremony in this Aztec codex picture. Aztec nobles played an important part in government. They were chosen by rulers to be judges, army commanders and officials. Nobles with government jobs paid no taxes and were given a free house to live in. Noblemen and women were born into ancient noble families, related to the rulers. It was, however, possible for an ordinary man to achieve higher rank if he fought very bravely in battle and captured four enemy soldiers alive.

WAR LEADER

This Maya stone carving shows ruler Shield Jaguar (*below left*) getting ready to lead his army in AD724. He is wearing a padded tunic and holding a knife in his right hand. His wife, Lady Xoc, is handing him his jaguar headdress. Maya rulers also took part in religious ceremonies, where they offered drops of their blood to the gods to ask for their help.

MEN AT WORK

Here, Aztec farmers are harvesting ripe cobs of maize. This painting comes from the Florentine Codex. This 12-volume manuscript was made by a Spanish friar. Codex pictures like this tell us a lot about ordinary peoples' everyday lives. Notice how simply the farmers are dressed compared to the more powerful people on these pages.

The Court, Government and Laws

Tᴴᴇ ʀᴇᴍᴀɪɴs ᴏғ ᴍᴀɴʏ splendid palaces survive in Mesoamerican lands. In the 1500s European explorers described the vast palace of the Aztec ruler Moctezuma II in Tenochtitlan. It had banqueting rooms big enough to seat 3,000 guests, private apartments, a library, a schoolroom, kitchens, stores, an arsenal for weapons, separate women's quarters, spectacular gardens and a large zoo. Etiquette around the emperor was very strict. Captains of the royal bodyguard had to approach Moctezuma barefoot, with downcast eyes, making low bows and murmuring, "Lord, my lord, my great lord." When they left, they had to walk backwards, keeping their gaze away from his face.

Palaces were not just rulers' homes. They were also official government headquarters where rulers greeted ambassadors from neighbouring city-states and talked with advisors.

Rulers also had the power to make strict laws. Each city-state had its own law-courts, where formidable judges had the power of life and death over people brought before them.

ROYAL RECORD
Maya rulers set up carved stone pillars in their cities to record major events during their reigns. These pillars are called stelae. This one celebrates a Maya ruler in Copan, Honduras.

Tʜᴇ Sᴇᴀᴛ ᴏғ Pᴏᴡᴇʀ
This carved jade ornament shows a seated Maya king. Although Aztec and Maya leaders had the final responsibility for decisions, they also relied on judges, officials and scribes to help them rule.

MAKE A FEATHER FAN

You will need: pencil, thick card, scissors, thin red card, green paper, double-sided tape, feathers (real or paper), masking tape, paints, paintbrushes, coloured felt, PVA glue and brush, sticky tape, coloured wool, bamboo cane.

1 Draw two rings about 45cm in diameter and 8cm wide on thick card. Cut them out. Make another ring the same size from thin red card, as above.

2 Cut lots of leaf shapes from green paper. Stick them around the edge of one thick card ring using double-sided tape. Add some real or paper feathers.

3 Cut two circles about 12cm in diameter from thin red card. Draw around something the right size, such as a reel of tape. These are for the centre of the fan.

LOCKED UP

Here, a group of Aztec judges discusses how to punish two prisoners. You can see them cowering in a wooden cage. By modern standards, punishments were very severe. If ordinary citizens broke the law, they might be beaten or speared with cactus spines. For a second offence, they might be stoned to death.

THE RULE OF THE GODS

This stone carving shows a human face being swallowed by a magic serpent. Royal and government buildings were often decorated with carvings such as this. They signified the religious power of the ruler of a particular city.

FIT FOR A KING

This picture from an Aztec codex shows visitors to a ruler's palace. It was reported by Spanish explorers that over six hundred nobles came to the Aztec ruler's palace every day to attend council meetings, consult palace officials, ask favours from the ruler and make their views heard. The ruler would sit on a mat on the floor with his council, as was the Aztec tradition.

Aztec nobles and rulers cooled themselves with beautiful feather fans.

4 Paint a flower on one of the two smaller red circles and a butterfly on the other. Cut v-shapes from the felt and glue them to the large red ring.

5 Using sticky tape, fix lengths of coloured wool to the back of one of the red circles, as shown. Place the red circle in the centre of the ring with leaves.

6 Tape the lengths of wool to the outer ring to look like spokes. Coat the ring with PVA glue and place the second card ring on top, putting a cane in between.

7 Use double-sided tape to stick the second red circle face up in the centre. Glue the red ring with felt v-shapes on top of the second thick card ring.

Family Life

Families were very important in Maya and Aztec times. By working together, family members provided themselves with food, jobs, companionship and a home. Each member of a family had special responsibilities. Men produced food or earned money to buy it. Women cared for babies and the home. From the age of about five or six, children were expected to do their share of the family's work by helping their parents. Because family life was so important, marriages were often arranged by a young couple's parents, or by a matchmaker. The role of matchmaker would be played by an old woman who knew both families well. Boys and girls got married when they were between 16 and 20 years old. The young couple usually lived in the boy's parents' home.

Aztec families belonged to local clan-groups, known as *calpulli*. Each *calpulli* chose its own leader, collected its own taxes and built its own temple. It offered help to needy families, but also kept a close eye on how members behaved. If someone broke the law, the whole clan might be punished for that person's actions.

MOTHER AND SON
These Maya clay figures may show a mother and her son. Boys from noble families went to school at about 15. They learned reading, writing, maths, astronomy and religion.

PAINFUL PUNISHMENT
This codex painting shows a father holding his son over a fire of burning chillies as a punishment. Aztec parents used severe punishments in an attempt to make their children honest and obedient members of society.

SPICE
Hot, spicy chilli peppers were an essential part of many Maya and Aztec meals. In fact, the Aztecs said that if a meal lacked chillies, it was a fast, not a feast! Chillies were used in stews and in spicy sauces, and they were used in medicine too. They were crushed and rubbed on aching muscles or mixed with salt to ease toothache.

red chillies

dried chillies, preserved for winter use

green chillies

IXTILTON

This Aztec mask is made of a black volcanic stone called obsidian. It shows the god Ixtilton, helper of Huitzilopochtli, the Aztecs' special tribal god. Aztec legends told how Ixtilton could bring darkness and peaceful sleep to tired children.

HUSBAND AND WIFE

The bride and groom in this codex picture of an Aztec wedding have their clothes tied together. This shows that their lives are now joined. Aztec weddings were celebrated with presents and feasting. Guests carried bunches of flowers, and the bride wore special make-up with her cheeks painted yellow or red. During the ceremony, the bride and groom sat side by side on a mat in front of the fire.

GUARDIAN GODDESS

The goddess Tlazolteotl is shown in this codex picture. She was the goddess of lust and sin. Tlazolteotl was also said to watch over mothers and young children. Childbirth was the most dangerous time in a woman's life, and women who died in childbirth were honoured like brave soldiers.

LEARNING FOR LIFE

A mother teaches her young daughter to cook in this picture from an Aztec codex. The girl is making tortillas, which are flat maize pancakes. You can see her grinding the corn in a *metate* (grinding stone) using a *mano* (stone used with the metate). Aztec mothers and fathers trained their children in all the skills they would need to survive in adult life. Children from the families of expert craftworkers learned their parents' special skills.

In the Home

MESOAMERICAN HOMES were not just safe places to eat and sleep. They were workplaces too. There were no refrigerators or household appliances, so women had to work hard preparing food for the day's meals or for winter storage. Vegetables were cleaned and chopped with stone knives, as there were no metal ones. Beans and chillies were spread out in the Sun to dry, and maize kernels were ground into flour. Homes had to be kept clean as well. Firewood and water had to be fetched and clothes washed. Women and girls spent long hours spinning thread and weaving it into cloth, then sewing it into tunics and cloaks for the family. Some women wove cloth to sell or to give to the government as a tax payment. Homes were also where most sick or elderly people were cared for.

HEART OF THE HOME
Throughout Mesoamerica, the hearth-fire was the heart of the home. This statue shows Xiuhtecuhtli, the Aztec god of fire. The top of his head is hollow, so a fire can be kindled there. The rays on his headdress represent flickering flames.

MAYA POT
The Maya decorated ceremonial pottery with pictures of gods, kings and important people. This pot shows a maize merchant. Pottery used in the home for food and drink would be less ornate.

A BACKSTRAP LOOM

You will need: paintbrush, water-based paint, 2 pieces of thick dowel about 70 cm long, string, scissors, thick card, masking tape, coloured wool.

1 Paint the pieces of dowel brown. Leave them to dry. Tie string to each dowel and wind it around. Leave a length of string loose at each end.

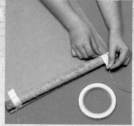

2 Cut a piece of thick card about 70cm x 100cm. This is a temporary base. Lightly fix the stringed dowels to it at the shorter sides with masking tape.

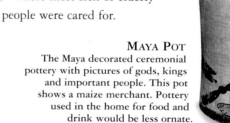

3 Now take your yellow wool. Thread the wool through the string loops and pull through to the other end, as shown. Try to keep the yellow wool taut.

GLOWING COLOURS

Many craftworkers worked at home. This painting by Diego Rivera shows craftworkers from the region of Tarascan dying hanks of yarn before they are woven into cloth. Mesoamerican dyes were made from fruits, flowers, shellfish and the cochineal beetles that lived on cactus plants. Only rich people were allowed to wear clothes made from brightly coloured cloth. Poorer people wore natural colours.

A HELPING HAND

Aztec girls were meant to make themselves useful by helping their mothers around the home. This Aztec codex picture shows a girl sweeping the floor with a bundle of twigs.

To weave, take the loom off the cardboard. Tie the loose string around your waist. Attach the other end of the loom to a post or tree with the string. Lean back to keep the long warp threads evenly taut.

WEAVING

Threads spun from plant fibres were woven into cloth on backstrap looms. The finest fabric was made from silky cotton. Rough yucca and cactus fibres made a coarser cloth. Looms like this are still used in Mexico today.

4 Cut a rectangle of thick card (300mm x 35mm). Now cut a small rectangle of card with one pointed end, as shown. Wind red wool around it.

5 Now take your long card rectangle. This is your shed rod. Carefully slide it through every second thread on your loom, as shown.

6 Turn your shed rod on its side. This will lift the threads up. Tie one end of your red wool to the yellow wool. Feed the card of wool through the lifted threads.

7 Lay the shed rod flat. Use the pointed end of your card to pick up each of the first or alternate threads. Thread the wool on the card through these.

Villages and Towns

MOST PEOPLE in Mesoamerica lived in country villages. They made a living from the land, taking their produce to nearby market towns to sell. Villages and towns all had to obey the strongest city in the region. Usually they also had to pay a tribute (a tax of goods or labour) to it as well. Villages were small, often with fewer than fifty families, but the biggest cities were huge. Historians estimate that over 150,000 people lived in the city of Teotihuacan in AD600. Cities, towns and villages were linked by roads cleared through the forest or by steep paths cut into mountain slopes.

The centre of most Mesoamerican cities was dedicated to religion. The greatest temples stood there, close to a vast open space used for holy ceremonies, dances and processions. Other important buildings, such as royal palaces and ball-courts, stood close by. The homes and workshops of ordinary citizens were built outside the ceremonial area.

HIDDEN IN THE TREES
Today the remains of the great Maya city of Tikal are almost hidden by the rainforest. In Maya times, the trees would have been felled to make room for houses and fields. In around AD800, about 50,000 people lived here.

DESERT FRUITS
Several kinds of cactus thrive in Mexico's dry, semi-desert, regions. The prickly pear had a sweet, juicy fruit, but the maguey cactus was even more useful. Its sap was used as a sweetener and to make an alcoholic drink. Its fibres were made into clothing and baskets. Its spines were used as needles.

BIG CITY
The Maya city of Copan in present-day Honduras covered an enormous area, perhaps 13km long and 3km wide. The religious centre and the nearby Great Plaza are shown here. Both were rebuilt in splendid style on the orders of King Yax Pac around AD750. The temples and royal palace are painted a glowing red – the colour of life and power.

BIRDS OF A FEATHER

These little pictures are from an Aztec codex. They show just some of the many beautiful wild birds that lived in Mesoamerica. The Maya and the Aztecs hunted many of them for their brightly coloured feathers. These feathers could then be used to make fans or shields.

humming bird

quetzal

toucan

parrot

parrot

MOUNTAINS AND MAIZE

On steep, cold mountain slopes, such as those of Popocatapetl, farmers grew hardy crops. *Chia* and *huautli* were both bushy plants with edible seeds. They were well suited to this environment. In sunny, fertile areas, maize was grown.

owl

crocodile

FROM DESERT TO RAINFOREST

The landscape of Mesoamerica is extremely varied. Many different creatures, from crocodiles to deer inhabit it. The Maya and the Aztecs hunted many of these animals for their meat or skins.

deer

butterfly

rabbit

snake

Buildings and Houses

PEOPLE LIVING in Mesoamerica used local materials for building. They had no wheeled transport, so carrying building materials long distances was quite difficult. Stone was the most expensive and longest-lasting building material. It was used for religious buildings, rulers' palaces and tombs. The homes of ordinary people were built more quickly and easily of cheaper materials, such as Sun-dried mud bricks, called adobe, or mud smeared over a framework of wooden poles. For strength, the walls might have stone foundations.

All Mesoamerican homes were very simply furnished. There were no chairs or tables, curtains or carpets – just some jars and baskets for storage and a few reed mats. Everyone, from rulers to slaves, sat and slept on mats on the floor. Most ordinary Aztec homes were L-shaped or built around a courtyard, with a separate bathroom for washing and a small shrine to the gods in the main room.

FAMILY HOME
This present-day Maya family home is built in traditional style, with red-painted mud-and-timber walls. It has one door and no windows. The floor is made of pounded earth. The roof, thatched with dried grass, is steeply sloped so the rain runs off it.

BURIED UNDERGROUND
Archaeologists have discovered these remains of houses at the Maya city of Copan. The roofs, walls and doors have rotted away, but we can still see the stone foundations. The houses are small and tightly packed together.

MAKE A MAYA HOUSE
You will need: thick card, pencil, ruler, scissors, glue, masking tape, terracotta plaster paste (or thin plaster coloured with paint), balsa wood strips, water pot, wide gummed paper tape, brush, short lengths of straw.

Back wall — 12cm — 20cm

Side wall — 12cm — 10cm

Side wall with fence — 12cm — 10cm — 16cm

Front of house — 12cm — 8cm — 6cm — 6cm — 10cm

Roof x 2 — 18cm — 23cm — 10cm

Side of roof x 2 — 10cm — 13cm

Draw the shapes of the roof and walls of the house on to thick card, using the measurements shown. (Please note that the templates are not shown to scale.) Cut the pieces out.

1 Cut out a rectangle 25cm x 15cm from thick card for the base. Stick the house walls and base together with glue. Use masking tape for support.

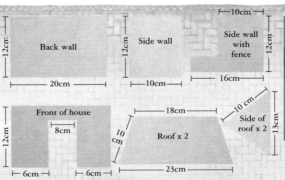

20

STONEMASONS AT WORK

Mesoamerican masons constructed massive buildings using very simple equipment. Their wedges were made from wood, and their mallets and hammers were shaped from hard volcanic stone. Until around AD900 metal tools were unknown. Fine details were added by polishing stonework with wet sand.

PLASTER

Big stone buildings, such as temples, were often covered with a kind of plaster called stucco. This was then painted with ornate designs. Plaster was made by burning limestone and mixing it with water and coloured earth. By the 1400s, there was so much new building in Tenochtitlan that the surrounding lake became polluted with chemicals from the plaster making.

plaster

limestone

SKILFUL STONEWORK

This carved stone panel from the Maya city of Chichen-Itza is decorated with a pattern of crosses. It was used to provide a fine facing to thick walls made of rubble and rough stone. This wall decorates a palace building.

A Maya house provided a cool shelter from the very hot Mexican Sun, as well as keeping out rain.

2 Paint the walls and base with plaster paste. This will make them look like Sun-dried mud. You could also decorate the doorway with balsa wood strips.

3 Put the house on one side to dry. Take your roof pieces and stick them together with glue. Use masking tape to support the roof, as shown.

4 Moisten the wide paper tape and use it to cover the joins between the roof pieces. There should be no gaps. Then cover the whole roof with glue.

5 Press lengths of straw into the glue on the roof. Work in layers, starting at the bottom. Overlap the layers. Fix the roof to the house using glue.

City in the Lake

THE AZTECS built their capital city, Tenochtitlan, on an island in the middle of Lake Texcoco in the Central Valley of Mexico. It was founded around AD1325 and soon grew into one of the largest cities in the world. Historians estimate that over 200,000 people lived there by 1500. As the centre of Aztec government, the city saw traders, ambassadors, scribes and porters streaming in with huge loads of tribute from all over Mesoamerica. Thousands of enemy soldiers captured in battle were also brought there to be sacrificed to the gods.

The city was divided into four districts – Flowery Place, Mosquito Fen, Herons' Home and, at the centre, the Sacred Precinct. The four districts of the city were linked to one another, and to the mainland, by countless little canals and causeways of pounded earth. These causeways ran above the surface of the lake. Fresh drinking water from the nearby mountains was carried by a tall stone acqueduct.

EAGLE AND CACTUS
According to legend, the Aztecs chose the site for Tenochtitlan after they received a message from the god Huitzilopochtli. He told them to build their city where they saw an eagle sitting on a cactus, eating a snake. Priests and rulers told legends like this to give reasons for their past actions and make people accept their future plans.

GIVING THANKS
The Aztecs decorated many parts of their city with images of their special god, Huitzilopochtli. Here we can see a brazier decorated with Huitzilopochtli's image, amongst the ruins of the great temple of Tenochtitlan.

EYE-WITNESS REPORTS
Today Tenochtitlan is buried under modern Mexico City. However, we can gain some idea of what it was like from drawings like this one, made by a European artist in the 1500s. It shows how causeways and canals allowed easy movement around the city.

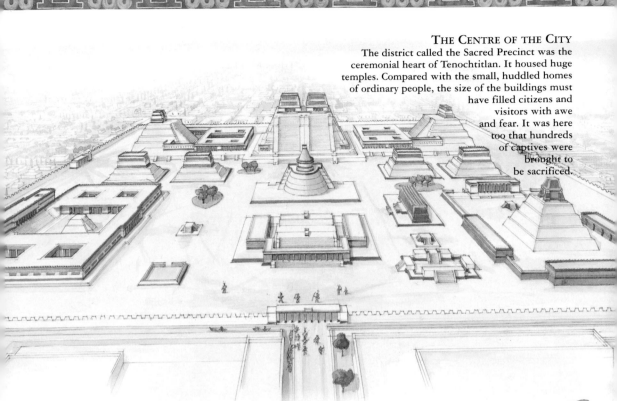

THE CENTRE OF THE CITY

The district called the Sacred Precinct was the ceremonial heart of Tenochtitlan. It housed huge temples. Compared with the small, huddled homes of ordinary people, the size of the buildings must have filled citizens and visitors with awe and fear. It was here too that hundreds of captives were brought to be sacrificed.

STONE WORSHIPPERS

These stone statues of standard bearers were found among the ruins of the Great Temple. This temple stood in the centre of Tenochtitlan. It had two tall pyramids, topped by shrines. These shrines were dedicated to Tlaloc, god of rain, and Huitzilopochtli, the Aztec's own special god of war. The remains of steps leading up to these shrines still remain. When the Spanish conquered the city, they pulled down the Great Temple and built a cathedral near the site.

THE LAKE OF THE MOON

This is the name the Aztecs gave to Lake Texcoco. This fanciful picture shows an 18th-century artist's idea of the Aztec ruler, Tenoch. This ruler founded the city of Tenochtitlan.

Farming

PEOPLE LIVING in different regions of Mesoamerica used various methods to cultivate their land. Farmers in the rainforests grew maize, beans and pumpkins in fields they cleared by slashing and burning. They cut down thick, tangled bushes and vines, leaving the tallest trees standing. Then they burned all the chopped-down bushes and planted seeds in the ashes. But the soil was only fertile for a few years. The fields were left to turn back into forest, and new ones were cleared. Maya farmers also grew crops in raised fields. These were plots of land along the edge of rivers and streams, heaped up with rich, fertile silt dug from the riverbed.

Aztec farmers planted maize wherever they could, on steep rocky hillsides and the flat valley floor. But they grew their biggest crops of fruit, flowers and vegetables in gardens called *chinampas*. These were reclaimed from the marshy shallows along the shores of Lake Texcoco and around the island city of Tenochtitlan.

MAIZE GOD
This stone statue shows Yum Caax (Lord of the Forest Bushes), the Maya god of maize. It was found at Copan. All Mesoamerican people honoured maize goddesses or gods, as the crop was so important.

DIGGING STICKS
Mesoamerican farmers had no tractors, horses or heavy ploughs to help them prepare their fields. Instead, a sharp-bladed wooden digging stick, called an *uictli*, was used for planting seeds and hoeing weeds. Some farmers in Mesoamerica today find digging sticks are more efficient than the kind of spade traditionally used in Europe.

FIELD WORK
This painting by Mexican artist Diego Rivera shows Aztecs using digging sticks to hoe fields of maize. You can see how dry the soil is. If the May rains failed, or frosts came early, a whole year's crop would be lost. Mesoamerican farmers made offerings to the rain god between March and October.

Chinampa soil was made even more fertile by using human manure.

Sticky mud was collected from the lake bottom. Along with compost and manure, this mud was poured on top of the chinampas.

The chinampa was held together by stakes, thick water vegetation and the tangled roots of trees.

FLOATING GARDENS

Chinampas were a sort of floating garden. They were made by sinking layers of twigs and branches under the surface of the lake and weighting them with stones. *Chinampas* were so productive that the government passed laws telling farmers when to sow seeds. This ensured there would be a steady supply of vegetables and flowers for sale in the market.

SLASH AND BURN

Mesoamerican farmers used a technique called slash and burn to clear land for farming. Crops grew very quickly in Mesoamerica's warm climate.

VEGETARIANS

Many ordinary Mesoamerican people survived on a largely vegetarian diet, based on maize and beans. This would be supplemented by other fresh fruits and vegetables in season. Meat and fish were expensive, luxury foods. Only rulers and nobles could afford to eat them every day.

FOREST FRUITS

This Aztec codex painting shows men and women gathering cocoa pods from trees. Cocoa was so valuable that it was sent as tribute to Tenochtitlan.

beans

prickly pear

Hunting and Gathering

MESOAMERICAN FARMERS did not rear many animals to kill for food. Before the Spaniards arrived, there were no cows, sheep, pigs or horses in their lands. Most meat and fish came from wild creatures, which were hunted or trapped. Deer, hares, rabbits and foxes were hunted on the dry mountain slopes. Peccary (wild boar), armadillos and opossums sheltered in the forests. Aztec hunters trapped ducks, geese and pelicans in shallow reed-beds beside the lake. Maya fishermen caught turtles, dolphins and shellfish all around the coast.

Hunters also went in search of many wild creatures that were not used for food. Millions of brightly-coloured birds were killed for their feathers. Poisonous snakes and fierce pumas, jaguars and ocelots (wild cats) were hunted for their beautiful furs and skins.

Mesoamerican people also gathered a great many plants and insects for other uses. Seeds, leaves, bark and flowers were used for medicine and to make paper, mats and baskets. Wild bees supplied honey, and locusts were eaten as snacks.

INSECT HARVEST
Mesoamerican people collected many kinds of insects for use in medicines, as dyes and as food. This codex picture shows cochineal beetles being gathered from a cactus. It took about 70,000 beetles to make half a kilo of red dye.

HUNTERS
Mesoamerican men went hunting with bows and arrows, slings, clubs and spears. Hunters' bows were made of wood, and their arrows were tipped with obsidian, a sharp volcanic glass. Their clubs were made from lumps of rock lashed to wooden handles with rope or leather thongs. To make their spears fly further, they used an *atlatl*. This was a grooved piece of wood that acted like an extra-long arm to increase the power behind the throw.

CHOCOLATE TREE

This picture from an Aztec codex shows a cocoa tree and two Aztec gods. Cocoa pods could be gathered from cocoa trees all over Mesoamerica. Once ground, the cocoa beans were mixed with water to make chocolate. Chocolate was a highly prized drink and only nobles could afford to drink it. It was often sweetened with honey and flavoured with vanilla. The Aztecs and Maya did not know how to make bars of solid chocolate, like those we enjoy today.

FAUNA

Wild creatures such as turtles, and rabbits were abundant in Mesoamerica. Rabbits were hunted for their fur. Turtles were a popular catch for many fishermen. Their shells could be used in crafts and their flesh could be eaten.

turtle *blacktail jackrabbit*

FEATHER TRADE

Mesoamerican merchants brought feathers from hunters who lived in the rainforest. The picture above shows different kinds of feathers sorted and ready for sale.

SEA PRODUCE

This Maya beaker is decorated with a picture of a god emerging from a shell. Beautiful seashells were highly prized in Mesoamerica and were often used in jewellery and craftwork. One species of shellfish was caught for its sticky slime. This slime was milked from the shellfish and then used to make a rich purple dye.

fishermen used sticks and paddles to drive fish into nets

flat-bottomed boats could sail across Mexico's shallow, marshy lakes

RIVERS AND LAKES

In this Aztec codex picture, we can see a boy fishing. He is standing in a flat-bottomed boat, hollowed from a single log. This boy is using a bag-shaped net, woven from cactus fibre. Fish were also caught with hooks, lines and harpoons. Long nets, draped across canoes, were used to catch waterfowl.

Food and Drink

MESOAMERICAN PEOPLE usually had two meals a day. They ate their main meal around noon and a smaller snack in the evening. Ordinary people's food was plain and simple but very healthy – if they could get enough of it. When crops failed, there was famine.

Everyday meals were based on maize, beans, vegetables and fruit. Peppers, tomatoes, pumpkins and avocado pears were popular vegetables, but the Aztecs also ate boiled cactus leaves (with the spines removed!). Gruel made from wild sage or amaranth seeds was also a favourite. Meat and fish were luxuries. Deer, rabbit, turkey and dog were cooked for feasts, along with frogs, lizards and turtles. The Aztecs also ate fish eggs and green algae from the lake.

USEFUL POTS

Mesoamerican people did not have metal cooking pots, so women cooked and served food in pottery bowls. Special pottery dishes were also used for specific jobs, such as cooking tortillas. The ones above were used for grating chillies and sweet peppers. They have rough ridged bases.

CACTUS WINE

Sweet, sticky sap from the maguey cactus was collected in leather flasks, then left to ferment in open troughs. It quickly turned into a strong alcoholic wine, which the Aztecs called *pulque*. Aztec men and women were not usually allowed to drink much alcohol. On special festivals honouring the dead, *pulque* was served by women wine-makers from huge pottery jars.

MAKE TORTILLAS

You will need: scales, 225g plain or maize flour, 1 tsp salt, bowl, 40g butter, jug, 120ml cold water, spoon, a little plain flour for kneading and flouring, rolling pin, pastry board, butter or oil for frying, frying pan.

1 Carefully weigh out the ingredients. If you cannot find maize flour, use plain flour instead. Aztec cooks had to grind their own flour.

2 Mix the flour and salt together in a bowl. Rub the butter into the mixture with your fingers until it looks like breadcrumbs. Then pour in the water.

3 Use your hands to mix everything together until you have a loose ball of dough. Do not worry if there is still some dry mixture around the bowl.

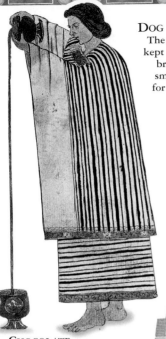

DOG FOOD
The Aztecs kept several breeds of small dog for eating.

CHOCOLATE
Maya cooks dried and pounded cocoa pod seeds into a thick paste. This was then boiled with water. To make the mixture smooth and frothy, they poured it from one bowl to another, often from a great height.

TORTILLAS AND TAMALES
This painting shows women grinding maize kernels into flour on a flat stone. They then shaped balls of raw dough into pancakes (tortillas) and stuffed dumplings (tamales). Tortillas were cooked on a hot baking-stone, while tamales were baked in a shallow dish.

NEW FOOD
In the years after the conquest of Mesoamerica, many vegetables were introduced to Europe, Asia and the Middle East. At first, gardeners found them difficult to grow, and cooks did not know how to prepare them. But today, many meals include tomatoes, peppers, chillies and avocado pears.

tomato *avocado pear*

You could eat your tortillas with spicy bean stew and juicy tomatoes, just like the Aztecs did.

4 Knead the dough for at least 10 minutes until it is smooth. If the dough or your hands get too sticky, add a little plain flour to the bowl.

5 Tip the dough out of the bowl on to a floured pastry board. Divide it into egg-sized balls, using your hands or a knife. You should have about 12 balls.

6 Sprinkle the board and the rolling pin with a little plain flour to stop the dough sticking. Then roll each ball of dough into a thin pancake shape.

7 Ask an adult to help you fry the tortillas, using a non-stick frying pan. Fry each tortilla for one minute per side. Use a little oil in the pan if you wish.

Keeping Healthy and Clean

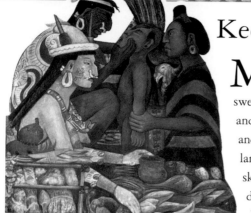

MESOAMERICAN PEOPLE liked to keep themselves and their houses clean. They washed in river water, took sweat-baths and swept their rooms with brushes of twigs and leaves. However, despite their attempts to stay clean and healthy, illness was common. Diseases recorded in Aztec lands, for example, include dysentery, chest infections and skin complaints. Throughout Mesoamerica, children often died from infections or in accidents around the home. Women died in childbirth, and many men were killed in battle. People were considered old by the time they were 40. Aztec medicine was a mixture of herbalism, religion, magic and first aid. Aztec doctors gave out powerful herbal medicines and encouraged patients to say prayers and make offerings to the gods. Sometimes their cures worked, but often the patients died.

DOCTOR ON CALL
A woman and child are shown consulting a doctor in the local market in this picture by Diego Rivera. The Aztecs made medicines out of many different fruits and herbs, some of which could kill or seriously damage the patient.

FOREIGN BODIES
Spanish settlers brought deadly diseases, such as measles and smallpox, to the Aztec and Maya lands in Mesoamerica after the conquest. Because of this the population of central Mexico fell from around 12 million in 1519 to only one million in 1600.

BURNING REMEDY
This scene from an Aztec codex advises people how to deal with fleas on their body. Pine resin was applied to the affected area and set alight. Patients could drink only cold water.

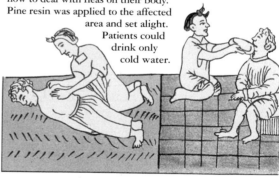

RASH MOMENT
A woman is shown treating an outbreak of sores on this man's skin. The patient would then drink and bathe in cactus sap.

HERBAL HEALTH

Many plants were cultivated or gathered for use in medicines. Their roots, seeds, leaves and resin could be used.

BREAK A LEG

To cure broken limbs, the Aztecs would grind various roots into a powder. These were placed on the break. A splint would then be tied to the broken limb.

AFTER CARE

The man shown here is recovering from a broken leg. After 20 days, a poultice of lime and powdered cactus root would be applied to his leg. When the leg was strong, the patient was advised to take a hot bath.

DEADLY BITES

Many dangerous creatures lived in the deserts and rainforests of Mesoamerica. Bites from dangerous spiders and venomous snakes were common hazards. Herbal remedies, such as the roots of a tree called rabbit fern, were used to treat bites and stings.

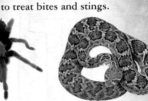

tarantula   *rattlesnake*

BROKEN SKULL

This man is suffering from a broken skull. The wound would be washed with urine to disinfect it.

COUGH MIXTURE

A persistent cough could be cured by an infusion of *teouaxin* cooked with chilli and salt.

BATHING ILLNESS AWAY

Steam baths like this were used for keeping clean. The Aztecs also used them to try to cure illness. They believed the baths would drive out the evil spirits that caused many diseases. Steam baths worked like a present-day sauna. Bathers sat in a small cabin, close to a fire, which heated large stones. When the stones were very hot, water was poured over them, creating clouds of steam.

Clothes, Hairstyles, Jewellery

AZTEC CLOTHES were very simple. Women wore a skirt and tunic, while men had a cloak and loincloth. But clothes still revealed a lot about the wearer. Strict laws described suitable clothing for different people. Ordinary families were meant to wear plain, knee-length clothes woven from rough *ixtle* (cactus fibre) and no jewellery. Nobles were allowed to wear longer-length clothes of fine white cotton, decorated with embroidery or woven patterns. They could also wear earrings, necklaces, labrets (lip-plugs) and bracelets of gold and precious stones. Maya clothes were also simple – just strips of fabric wound around the body. Maya ideas of beauty would be strange to us. They filed their teeth and encouraged their children to grow up cross-eyed. Mothers also bound their babies' heads to flatten them.

GLITTERING GOLD
This gold chest ornament is in the shape of a skeleton-faced god. It was made by Mixtec goldsmiths from southern Mexico. Jewellery was worn only by nobles. In Mesoamerica, both noblemen and women wore fine jewellery.

CEREMONIAL CLOTHES
Musicians and actors walk in procession in this picture. It is copied from a wall painting in a Maya ruler's palace at Bonampak. The procession forms part of a celebration to honour the ruler's child. The men on the right are wearing white cloth headdresses and wrap-around skirts, tied with sashes at the waist.

MAKE A BAT BROOCH

You will need: pencil, thin card, scissors, black and gold paint, small paintbrush, paint pot, palette, glue, glue brush, string, small safety pin, masking tape.

1 Draw the shape of your brooch in pencil on thin card (6cm x 10cm). This brooch is based on a gold Aztec pendant shaped like a vampire bat god.

2 Carefully cut out the finished shape with scissors. Aztec jewellery designs were very delicate and complicated. They often featured gods.

3 Use black paint to colour in the eyes, mouth and hair of your bat, as shown above. It is best to use the paint fairly thickly.

CLOAK AND DAGGER

This Aztec warrior is wearing a long, brightly coloured cloak and an elaborate feather headdress. Aztec cloaks were simple rectangles of cloth, fastened at the shoulder by a knot. There were strict rules governing their length. Only nobles or soldiers who had legs that had been badly scarred in battle could wear cloaks like this one, coming below the knee. Ordinary men had to wear short cloaks.

MEXICAN STYLE

A Huastec woman from Veracruz, on the north coast of Mexico, is shown in this statue. She is wearing a wide tunic and a long skirt. Her hair is tied up in a carefully-folded headdress, and she wears a necklace and disk-shaped earrings. Although different patterns were favoured by the peoples of the various Mesoamerican cultures, the style of clothing was essentially very similar.

SKIRTS, TUNICS AND CLOAKS

A well-off Aztec couple sit by the fire, while their hostess cooks a meal. Both women are wearing long skirts. The bright embroidery of their tunics is a sign of high rank. Their long hair is braided and tied on top of their heads to make horns in a typical married woman's style. Girls and unmarried women wore their hair loose down their backs.

4 Cut teeth out of card and glue in place. Use the glue to stick string on the bat's face, head and body. Coil the string into spirals for the hair. Leave to dry.

5 Carefully paint the brooch all over (except for the black areas) with gold paint. Leave in a warm place for the paint to dry.

6 When the paint is dry, turn the brooch over and fix a safety pin on to the back with masking tape. Make sure it is secure.

You could wear your brooch on your chest, as the Aztecs did, or pin it on your sleeve.

Craftworkers

SPANISH EXPLORERS arriving in Mesoamerica were amazed at the wonderful objects they found there. They were better than anything they had seen in Europe. Pottery, jewellery, fabrics, mosaics, masks, knives and feather work were all made by skilled Mesoamerican craftworkers using simple, hand-powered tools. In big cities such as Tenochtitlan, Aztec craftworkers organized themselves into guilds. These made sure that all members worked to the highest standards and trained new workers. Many craft skills were passed from parents to children. Sometimes whole families worked as a team in workshops next to the family home.

Many Mesoamerican craft goods were decorated with beautiful patterns. Often, they had special religious meanings. Aztec warriors marched into battle carrying magic feathered shields. Jewellery was decorated with death's-head designs. Many Maya rulers and nobles were buried with elaborately decorated pots.

MOSAIC MASK
This ritual mask is inlaid with a mosaic of turquoise. This valuable stone was brought back from mines in North America by Aztec traders.

LIVING JEWELS
Featherworkers wove or glued thousands of feathers together to make headdresses, cloaks, warriors' uniforms, shields and fans. Men drew the designs on stiffened cloth and made light wooden frames to support the finished item. Women cleaned and sorted the feathers.

MAKE A MOSAIC MASK
You will need: balloon, petroleum jelly, newspaper, papier-mâché mixture (1 part PVA glue to 3 parts water), bowl, paintbrush, scissors, gummed paper tape, palette of paints, water pot, self-drying clay, card, plaster coloured with paint.

1 Inflate a balloon to the size of your head. Cover with petroleum jelly. Soak strips of newspaper in papier-mâché mixture. Add five layers to the front of the balloon.

2 Once dry, pop the balloon. Draw a mask shape on to the papier-mâché and cut it out. Use clay to add eyes and a nose. Cover the edges with gummed paper. Leave to dry.

3 Mix white and blue paint together to create three different shades. Paint one sheet of card with each. When dry, cut them into little pieces.

WARRIOR DISH

This dish was made in the Maya city of Tikal, in present-day Guatemala. It is painted with slip (a liquid clay coloured with minerals) and shows the figure of a warrior. All Mesoamerican pots were shaped by hand – the use of a potter's wheel was not known.

WOVEN TRIBUTE

Cloaks and blankets were sent as tribute to the great city of Tenochtitlan, as well as being sold in markets.

MOULDING GOLD

This painting by Diego Rivera shows Aztec goldsmiths with molten gold. Most jewellery was made by melting gold-dust in a furnace, then pouring it into a mould.

TREASURES

Mesoamerican people treasured many beautiful semi-precious stones, such as turquoise, obsidian and rock-crystal. They paid high prices for corals, pearls and shells from the sea. But they valued jade, a hard, smooth, deep-green stone, most of all, because it symbolized eternal life.

turquoise   *obsidian*

Aztec craftworkers carefully cut semi-precious stones into tiny squares. Turquoise, jade, shell and obsidian were all used for this purpose. The craftworkers used these pieces to create beautiful mosaic masks like this.

4 Cover the mask (except the eyes and mouth) with plaster paste. Press the card pieces into this, using glue to help any awkward ones to stick.

5 Paint the eyes with black and white paint. Cut out teeth from white card and carefully glue in position. Leave the mask in a warm place to dry.

6 Now coat the whole mask with a thin coat of PVA glue. This will seal the surface of the mask.

Merchants and Markets

THE MARKET PLACE was the heart of many Mesoamerican cities and towns. Traders, craftworkers and farmers met there to exchange their produce. Many market traders were women. They sold cloth or cooking pots, made by themselves or their families, and maize, fruit, flowers and vegetables grown by their husbands. In big cities, such as the trading centre of Tlatelolco, government officials also sold exotic goods that had been sent to the Aztec rulers as tribute (taxes) by conquered city-states. After the Aztecs conquered Tlatelolco in 1473, it soon became the greatest market in Mesoamerica. It was reported that almost 50,000 people came there on the busiest days.

Long-distance trade was carried out by merchants called *pochteca*. Gangs of porters carried their goods. The work was often dangerous, but the rewards were great.

MERCHANT GOD

Yacatecuhtli was the Aztec god of merchants and traders. In the codex picture above, he is shown standing in front of a crossroads marked with footprints. Behind him (*right*), is a tired porter with a load of birds on his back.

MAIZE MARKET

Mesoamerican farmers grew many different varieties of maize, with cobs that were pale cream, bright yellow, or even deep blue. Their wives took the maize to market, as selling was women's work. This modern wall-painting shows Aztec women buying and selling maize in the great market at Tlatelolco. At the market, judges sat in raised booths, keeping a lookout for thieves and cheats.

MAKE A MAYA POT

You will need: self-drying clay, board, rolling pin, masking tape, modelling tool, water bowl, small bowl, petroleum jelly, PVA glue, glue brush, yellow and black paint, paintbrush, water pot.

1 Roll out the clay until it is approximately 5mm thick. Cut out a base for the pot with a modelling tool. Use a roll of masking tape as a guide for size.

2 Roll out some long sausages of clay. Coil them around the base of the pot to build up the sides. Join and smooth the clay with water as you go.

3 Model a lip at the top of the pot. Leave it to dry. Cover a small bowl with petroleum jelly. Make a lid by rolling out some clay. Place the clay over the bowl.

JOURNEY'S END

This modern painting shows merchants and porters arriving at the market city of Tlatelolco. Such travellers made long journeys to bring back valuable goods, such as shells, jade and fig-bark paper. Young men joining the merchants' guild were warned about tiredness, pain and ambushes on their travels.

SKINS

Items such as puma, ocelot and jaguar skins could fetch a high price at market.

BARTER

Mesoamerican people did not have coins. They bought and sold by bartering, exchanging the goods they wanted to sell for other peoples' goods of equal value. Costly items such as gold-dust, quetzal feathers and cocoa beans were exchanged for goods they wanted to buy.

colourful feathers   *cocoa beans*

MARKET PRODUCE

In Mexico today, many markets are still held on the same sites as ancient ones. Many of the same types of foodstuffs are on sale there. In this modern photograph, we see tomatoes, avocados and vegetables that were also grown in Aztec times. Today, as in the past, most market traders and shoppers are women.

Mesoamerican potters made their pots by these coil or slab techniques. The potter's wheel was not used at all in Mesoamerica. The pots were sold at the local market.

4 Turn your pot upside down and place it over the rolled-out clay. Trim away the excess clay with a modelling tool by cutting around the top of the pot.

5 Use balls of clay to make a turtle to go on top of the lid. When both the lid and turtle are dry, use PVA glue to stick the turtle on to the centre of the lid.

6 Roll three small balls of clay of exactly the same size for the pot's feet. When they are dry, glue them to the base of the pot. Make sure they are evenly spaced.

7 Paint the pot with Aztec designs in black and yellow. When you have finished, varnish the pot with a thin coat of PVA glue to make it shiny.

Travel and Transport

MESOAMERICAN PEOPLE knew about wheels but they did not make wheeled transport of any kind. Carriages and carts would not have been suitable for journeys through dense rainforests or along steep, narrow mountain tracks. Many Maya cities were also linked by raised causeways that would have been difficult for wheeled vehicles to travel along.

Most people travelled overland on foot, carrying goods on their backs. Mesoamerican porters carried heavy loads with the help of a *tumpline*. This was a broad band of cloth that went across their foreheads and under the bundles on their backs, leaving their arms free. Rulers and nobles were carried in beds, called litters.

On rivers and lakes, Mesoamericans used simple dug-out boats. At sea, Maya sailors travelled in huge wooden canoes that were able to make voyages of many kilometres in rough seas.

CARRIED HIGH
A Maya nobleman is shown being carried in a litter (portable bed) made from jaguar skins. Spanish travellers reported that the Aztec emperor was carried in the same way. Blankets were also spread in front of the emperor as he walked, to stop his feet touching the ground.

MEN OR MONSTERS?
Until the Spaniards arrived with horses in 1519, there were no animals big and strong enough to ride in the Mesoamerican lands. There were horses in America in prehistoric times, but they died out around 10,000BC. When the Aztecs saw the Spanish riding, they thought they were monsters – half man, half beast.

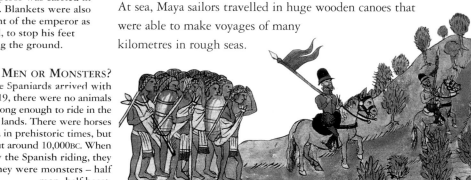

A WHEELED DOG

You will need: board, self-drying clay, 4 lengths of thin dowel about 5cm long and 2 lengths about 7cm long, water bowl, modelling tool, thick card, scissors, PVA glue, glue brush, paintbrush, modelling tool, paintbrush, paint, masking tape.

1 Roll a large piece of clay into a fat sausage to form the dog's body. Push the 5cm pieces of dowel into the body to make the legs. Leave to dry.

2 Cover the dowel legs with clay, extending the clay 2cm beyond the end of the dowel. Make a hole at the end of each leg with a piece of dowel. Leave to dry.

3 Push the dowel through the holes in the legs to join them horizontally. Make the dog's head and ears from clay. Join them to the body using water.

HARDWORKING PORTERS

This engraving from the 1900s shows Aztec slaves and commoners carrying loads for Spanish conquerors. Being a porter was very hard work. They were expected to cover up to 100 km per day, carrying about 25–30kg on their backs. Like most Mesoamerican people, they travelled these long distances barefoot.

BY BOAT

Aztec soldiers and the citizens of Tenochtitlan used boats with flat bottoms to travel around the city. Boats like this were also used to carry fruits and vegetables to market. Dug-out canoes were popular too. They were made from hollowed out tree trunks.

AZTEC WATERWAYS

The Aztecs paddled their canoes and flat-bottomed boats on Lake Texcoco. Today most of this lake has dried up. The lakeside *chinampas*, where they grew food and flowers, have almost disappeared. This photograph shows modern punts sailing along one of the last remaining Aztec waterways between the few *chinampas* that survive.

Toys like this dog are proof that the wheel was known in Mesoamerica. Wheeled vehicles were not suitable for rugged Mesoamerican land.

4 Cut four circles 3.5cm in diameter from card to make wheels. Pierce a hole in the centre of each. Make the holes big enough for the dowel to fit through

5 Make four wheels from clay, the same size as the card wheels. Glue the clay and card wheels together. Make holes through the clay wheels and leave to dry.

6 Paint the dog's head, body, legs and wheels with Aztec patterns. When the paint is dry, give the dog a thin coat of PVA glue to act as a varnish.

7 Fit the wheels on to the ends of the dowels that pass through the dog's legs. Wrap strips of masking tape around the ends to stop the wheels falling off.

Warriors and Weapons

AZTEC ARMIES were very large. All Aztec men learned how to fight and had to be ready to hurry off to battle when they heard the sound of the great war drum outside the ruler's palace in Tenochtitlan. Ordinary soldiers wore tunics and leg-guards of padded cotton that had been soaked in saltwater. This made it tough – strong enough to protect the wearer from many fierce blows. Aztec army commanders wore splendid uniforms decorated with gold, silver, feathers and fur.

Both the Maya and the Aztecs greatly admired bravery. Aztec armies were led by nobles who had won promotion for brave deeds in battle, or for taking lots of captives. It was a disgrace for an Aztec soldier to try to save his own skin. It was more honourable for him to be killed fighting, or to be sacrificed, than to survive.

Maya soldiers went to war to win captives for sacrifice, but they also fought battles to control trade routes, to obtain tribute and to gain power. They wore a variety of garments, including sleeveless tunics, loincloths, fur costumes and cotton armour.

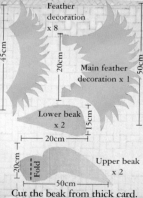

TOLTEC WARRIORS
A proud warrior stands at Tula, the capital city of the Toltec people. He wears a butterfly-shaped breastplate. Butterflies have short but brilliant lives. For the Toltecs, they were a symbol of brave warriors and early death. The Toltecs were famous for their battle skills throughout Aztec and Maya lands.

HELD CAPTIVE
An Aztec warrior is shown capturing an enemy in battle in this codex picture. The warrior is dragging his captive along by the hair. Young Aztec men had to grow their hair long at the back and could only cut it when they had taken their first prisoner in battle.

AN EAGLE HELMET

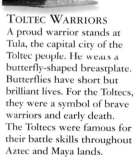

You will need: ruler, thick card, pencil, scissors, masking tape, stapler, self-drying clay, PVA glue, glue brush, gummed paper tape, paints, paintbrush, water pot, ribbon, felt, green paper, Velcro.

Feather decoration x 8

45cm

20cm

Main feather decoration x 1

50cm

Lower beak x 2

15cm

20cm

20cm

Fold

Upper beak x 2

50cm

Cut the beak from thick card. Cut the feathers from paper.

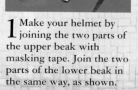

1 Make your helmet by joining the two parts of the upper beak with masking tape. Join the two parts of the lower beak in the same way, as shown.

2 Fold the two rounded ends of the upper beak towards each other and staple them together. Cover the staples and the join with masking tape.

JAGUAR AND EAGLE KNIGHTS

Ocelotl, the jaguar, is shown in this picture from a codex. Warriors had to prove their bravery in battle and capture lots of prisoners for sacrifice. Those who succeeded were invited to join special fighting brotherhoods of jaguar and eagle knights. They wore costumes made of real feathers and skins.

WARRIOR SPIRIT

This stone carving is from the Maya city of Yaxchilan. In it, Lady Xoc, wife of ruler Shield Jaguar, kneels before a vision serpent. This serpent was made to appear by a special religious ritual. Maya rulers made offerings of their own blood to their ancestor-spirits and to the gods to ask for help in battle.

CLUBS AND SPEARS

Aztec soldiers face Spanish soldiers on horseback. They are armed with war-clubs called *macuahuitl* and protected by wooden shields. War-clubs, made of wood and razor-sharp flakes of obsidian, could cut an enemy's head off with a single blow. The Spaniards are armed with metal swords and lances.

Fasten your eagle helmet by tying it under the chin. You could make wings from card and attach them to your arms with ribbon. Now you are a brave eagle knight! Eagles were admired by the Aztecs as superb hunters who could move freely to the Sun.

3 Make two eyes from self-drying clay and stick them on to the upper beak with glue. Neaten the edges of the beak and eyes with gummed paper tape.

4 Decorate both parts of the beak with paint. If you wish, add pieces of ribbon, felt or paper, too. Remember that you want to look brave and fierce.

5 Ask an adult to curl the feathers by running a scissor blade along them. Glue the layers of feathers on to the main feather decoration. Trim to fit.

6 Use tape and glue to fix feathers to the inside of the upper beak. Tape ribbon from the upper beak to the lower one to join. Leave some ribbon loose to tie.

Rival City-States

TIKAL
This figure was painted on a pottery vase from the city of Tikal. From about AD600 to 900, Tikal was one of the greatest Maya city-states. It was wealthy, busy and very big. About 75,000 people lived there, and its buildings covered an area of 100 square kilometres. Around AD400, Tikal conquered the nearby Maya state of Uaxactun. Trading and religious links were then developed with the powerful non-Maya city of Teotihuacan.

THE MAYA LIVED in many separate city-states, which were always rivals and sometimes at war. Rulers of different states fought to win more land. From around AD200, they also competed with one another to fill their cities with bigger, more beautiful buildings.

They competed over political power, control of land and resources, and trade routes.

Between about AD850 and AD900, many Maya cities became poorer, and their power collapsed. The great city centres were abandoned, and Maya scribes and craftworkers no longer carved important dates on temples and tombs. The last date known is AD889. No one knows why this happened. Perhaps it was because of famine, caused by bad weather or farmers over-using the land, or it may have been caused by war. However, Maya civilization did not totally disappear. A few Maya cities, in the far north and south of Mexico, continued to thrive.

Around AD900, the Putun people from the Gulf coast moved into Maya lands. In cities like Chichen-Itza, Putun ideas blended with Maya traditions to create a new culture.

CHICHEN-ITZA
Pilgrims came from miles around to throw jewellery and fine pottery into the Well of Sacrifice in the city of Chichen-Itza. These items were offerings to the god of rain. Human sacrifices were made here too. Chichen-Itza was founded by the Maya around AD800. Later, Maya craftsmen built a massive new city centre, with temples and ball-courts. Many of these new buildings were based on designs similar to those found in central Mexico. Some historians think this means that the city was conquered by the Putuns.

UXMAL

The city of Uxmal is in the dry Puuc region of Yucatan, Mexico. There are no rivers or streams in the area, so Maya engineers designed and built huge underground tanks, called *chultun*, to store summer rainfall. People living in Uxmal relied on these water tanks for survival.

NAMES AND DATES

This stone slab was once placed above a doorway in the Maya city of Yaxchilan. It is carved with glyphs, or picture-symbols, recording important names and dates. The city of Yaxchilan is famous for the fine quality stone carvings found there, especially on tall pillars and around doors.

PALENQUE

Lord Pacal, ruler of the Maya city of Palenque, was buried wearing this mask of green jade. Only the richest city-states could afford to bury their rulers with treasures like this. Palenque was at its strongest between AD600 and 800.

COPAN

This stela (tall stone pillar) is from Copan in modern Honduras. The front of the stela is carved with a larger-than-life portrait of 18 Rabbit (Waxaklahun ubah k'awil), the thirteenth ruler of the city. Archaeologists know much about Copan's past from the inscriptions carved in several monuments and buildings.

Aztec Conquests

TOTONAC TRIBUTE
Ambassadors from lands conquered by the Aztecs came to Tenochtitlan to deliver the tribute demanded from their rulers. This painting shows splendidly dressed representatives of the Totonac people meeting Aztec tax collectors. The Totonacs lived on the Gulf coast of Mexico, in Veracruz. Here they are shown offering tobacco, fruit and vanilla grown on their lands. They hated and feared the Aztecs.

W AR WAS ESSENTIAL to Aztec life. As newcomers in Mexico, the Aztecs had won their homeland by fighting against the people already living there. From then onwards, they relied on war to bring more land, new cities and extra tribute under their control. Without these riches won through war, the Aztec empire would have collapsed. Big cities such as Tenochtitlan needed steady supplies of tribute to feed their citizens. War was also a source of captives. The Aztecs believed that thousands of prisoners needed to be sacrificed each year.

Each new Aztec ruler had to start his reign with a battle. It was his duty to win fame and glory by conquering new territory and seizing enemy captives. During the 1400s, the Aztec empire grew rapidly, until the Aztecs ruled most of Mexico. This drive to conquer new territory was led by rulers Itzcoatl (1426–1440), Moctezuma Ilhuicamina (1440–1468) and Axayacatl (1468–1481). Conquered cities were often controlled by garrisons of Aztec soldiers and linked to the government in Tenochtitlan by large numbers of officials, such as tax collectors and scribes.

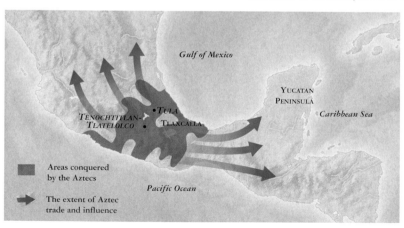

Gulf of Mexico

YUCATAN PENINSULA

Caribbean Sea

TENOCHTITLAN-
TLATELOLCO

TULA

TLAXCALLA

Pacific Ocean

Areas conquered by the Aztecs

The extent of Aztec trade and influence

AZTEC LANDS
This map shows the area ruled by the Aztecs in 1519. Conquered cities were allowed to continue with their traditional way of life, but had to pay tribute to Aztec officials. The Aztecs also put pressure on two weaker city states, Texcoco and Tlacopan, to join with them in a Triple Alliance. One nearby city-state, Tlaxcalla, refused to make an alliance with the Aztecs and stayed fiercely independent.

CANNIBALS

One of the Aztecs' most important reasons for fighting was to capture prisoners for sacrifice. In this codex picture, we can see sacrificed bodies neatly chopped up. In some religious ceremonies, the Aztecs ate the arms and legs of sacrificed prisoners.

FROM HUMBLE BEGINNINGS

Aztec settlers are shown on their difficult trek through northern Mexico. The Aztecs built up their empire from humble beginnings in a short time. They first arrived in Mexico some time after AD1200. By around 1400, they had become the strongest nation in central Mesoamerica. To maintain their position, they had to be ready for war. The Aztecs invented many legends to justify their success. They claimed to be descended from earlier peoples living in Mexico, and to be specially guided by the gods.

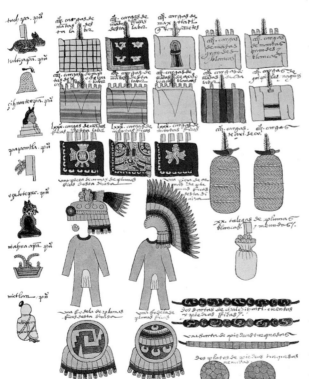

TRIBUTE LIST

The Aztecs received vast quantities of valuable goods as tribute each year. Most of the tribute was sent to their capital city of Tenochtitlan. Aztec scribes there drew up very detailed lists of tribute received, like the one on the left. Among the goods shown are shields decorated with feathers, blankets, turquoise plates, bracelets and dried chilli peppers.

Scholars and Scribes

THE MAYA were the first — and only — Native American people to invent a complete writing system. Maya picture-symbols and sound-symbols were written in books, carved on buildings, painted on pottery and inscribed on precious stones. Maya scribes also developed an advanced number system, including a sign for zero, which Europeans at the time did not have.

Maya writing used glyphs (pictures standing for words) and also picture-signs that stood for sounds. The sound-signs could be joined together, like the letters of our alphabet, to spell out words and to make complete sentences. The Aztecs used picture-writing too, but theirs was much simpler and less flexible.

Maya and Aztec picture-symbols were very difficult to learn. Only specially trained scribes could write them and only priests or rich people could read them. They could spare time for study and afford to pay a good teacher.

MAYA READER
This Maya statue shows a wealthy woman, seated cross-legged with a codex (folding book), on her lap. A Maya or Aztec codex was made of long strips of fig-bark paper, folded like a concertina. The writing was read from top to bottom and left to right.

CITY EMBLEM
This is the emblem-glyph for the Maya city-state of Copan. It is made up of four separate images, which together give a message meaning "the home of the rulers of the royal blood of Copan". At the bottom, you can see a bat, the special picture-sign for the city.

MAKE A CODEX
You will need: thin card, ruler, pencil, scissors, white acrylic paint, eraser, large and small paintbrushes, water pot, paints in red, yellow, blue and black, palette, tracing paper.

1 Draw a rectangle about 100cm x 25cm on to thin card. Cut the rectangle out. Cover it evenly with white acrylic paint. Leave it to dry.

2 Using a pencil and ruler, lightly draw in four fold-lines 20cm apart. This will divide the painted card into five equal sections.

3 Carefully fold along the pencil lines to make a zig-zag book, as shown. Unfold the card and rub out the pencil lines with an eraser.

MAYA CODEX

Maya scribes wrote thousands of codices, but only four survive. All the rest were destroyed by Spanish missionaries. These pages from a Maya codex show the activities of several different gods. The figure at the top painted black with a long nose is Ek Chuah, the god of merchants.

zero   *one*   *four*   *five*   *eleven*   *eighteen*

AZTEC ENCYCLOPEDIA

These pictures of Aztec gods come from a book known as the Florentine Codex. This encyclopedia was compiled between 1547 and 1569 by Father Bernardino de Sahagun, a Spanish friar. He was fascinated by Aztec civilization and wanted to record it before it disappeared. This codex is the most complete written record of Aztec life we have.

MAYA NUMBERS

The Maya number system used only three signs – a dot for one, a bar for five, and the shell-symbol for zero. Other numbers were made by using a combination of those signs. When writing down large numbers, Maya scribes put the different symbols on top of one another, rather than side by side as we do today.

4 Trace or copy Aztec or Maya codex drawings from this book. Alternatively, make up your own, based on Mesoamerican examples.

5 Paint your tracings or drawings, using light, bright colours. Using the Maya numbers on this page as a guide, add some numbers to your codex.

If you went to school in Aztec or Maya times, you would find out how to recognize hundreds of different picture-symbols. You would also be taught to link them together in your mind, like a series of clues, to find out what they meant.

Time, Sun and Stars

Like all other Mesoamericans, the Maya and the Aztecs measured time using a calendar with a year of 260 days. This was used in Mexico as early as 500BC and is probably based on human biology – 260 days is about how long it takes a baby to develop before it is born. The calendar was divided into 13 cycles of 20 days each. Mesoamerican farmers used a different calendar, based on the movements of the Sun, because sunlight and the seasons made their crops grow. This calendar had 360 days, divided into 18 months of 20 days, plus five extra days that were unlucky. Every 52 years, measured in our time, these two calendars ended on the same day. For five days before the end of the 52 years, people were anxious, because they feared the world might end. A third calendar, of 584 days, also existed for calculating festival days.

SUN STONE
This massive carving was made to display the Aztec view of creation. The Aztecs believed that the world had already been created and destroyed four times and that their Fifth World was also doomed.

STUDYING THE STARS
The Caracol was constructed as an observatory to study the sky. From there, Maya astronomers could observe the planet Venus, which was important in the Mesoamericans' measurement of time.

MAKE A SUN STONE

You will need: pencil, scissors, thick card, self-drying clay, modelling tool, board, rolling pin, masking tape, PVA glue, glue brush, water bowl, pencil, thin card, water-based paints, paintbrush, water pot.

1 Cut a circle about 25cm in diameter from thick card. Roll out the clay and cut out a circle, using the card as a guide. Place the clay circle on the card one.

2 With a modelling tool, mark a small circle in the centre of the clay circle. Use a roll of masking tape as a guide. Do not cut through the clay.

3 Carve the Sun-god's eyes, mouth, teeth and earrings. You can use the real Aztec Sun stone, shown at the top left of this page, as a guide.

alligator

wind

house

lizard

NAMES OF DAYS

These pictures from an Aztec codex show the 20 names for days from the farmers' calendar. These symbols were combined with a number from one to 13 to give the date, such as Three Vulture. The days were named after familiar creatures or everyday things, such as the lizard or water. Each day also had its own god. Children were often named after the day on which they were born, a custom that still continues in some parts of Mexico up to the present day.

serpent

death's head

deer

rabbit

Water

dog

monkey

grass

Your finished Sun stone will not be as big as the original Aztec one. That measures four metres across and is the largest Aztec sculpture discovered so far.

reed

jaguar

eagle

vulture

motion

flint knife

rain

flower

4 Roll out more clay and cut out some Sun's rays, a tongue and eyebrows. Glue them to the clay circle. Smooth the edges with water and leave to dry.

5 Copy the 20 Aztec symbols (*above*) for days on to squares of thin card. The card squares should be no more than 2cm x 2cm. Cut out. Paint brown.

6 Cover the clay circle with a thin coat of dark brown paint. Leave it to dry. Then add a thin coat of white paint to make the circle look like stone.

7 Glue the card symbols evenly around the edge of the clay circle, as shown. Paint the Sun stone with a thin layer of PVA glue to seal and varnish it.

Gods and Goddesses

RELIGION WAS a powerful force throughout Mesoamerica. It affected everything people did, from getting up in the morning to digging in their fields or obeying their ruler's laws. Everyone believed that the gods governed human life. People could not fight their decisions, but the gods could sometimes be persuaded to grant favours if they were offered gifts and sacrifices. The Aztecs and Maya believed in ancient nature gods such as the fire god, the god of maize and the god of rain, and worshipped them with splendid festivals and ceremonies. Mesoamerican people also honoured the spirits of their dead rulers. The Aztecs had their own special tribal god, Huitzilopochtli, Lord of the Sun. He rewarded his followers with victories in war.

Religious ceremonies and sacrifices were led by temple priests. With long, matted hair, red-rimmed eyes and their painted bodies splattered with blood, they were a terrifying sight.

GOD OF SPRING
Xipe Totec was the Aztec god of fertility. He protected the young shoots of maize. Each year, captives were skinned alive as a sacrifice to him. Priests dressed in their skins in religious ceremonies to remind everyone of the skin of young plants.

CHACMOOL FIGURE
This stone statue from the city of Chichen-Itza shows a Chacmool, or reclining figure. It is holding a stone slab on which offerings may have been made.

A STATUE OF A GOD

You will need: pencil, paper, self-drying clay, modelling tool, pastry board, water bowl, petroleum jelly, cotton-wool bud, plaster of Paris, terracotta paint, small paintbrush.

1 Make a drawing of any Aztec god. Model it as a flat figure from self-drying clay. Keep it flat on the bottom. Leave the clay figure to dry.

2 Completely cover the surface of your model with petroleum jelly. Then smooth a layer of clay over the jelly, pressing it down gently into any grooves.

3 Spread more clay on top to make a strong rectangular block, at least 3cm thick. This will become your mould. Leave it to dry thoroughly.

WATER AND RAIN

Tlaloc was the Aztec god of life-giving rain, "the god who makes things grow". Under different names, he was worshipped throughout Mesoamerica. Tlaloc was honoured when he sent water to nourish the crops and feared when he sent deadly floods. In times of drought, the Aztecs sacrificed babies to Tlaloc. They believed the babies' tears would make rain fall.

SUN AND JAGUAR

This Maya carving was part of a wall at Campeche in south-eastern Mexico. It shows the Sun god, whom the Maya called Kinich Ahau. The Maya believed that he disappeared into the underworld every night, at sunset. It was there that he turned into a fierce jaguar god. At the beginning of every new day, they believed that Kinich Ahau then returned to Earth as the life-giving Sun.

EARTH MOTHER

This huge statue of Coatlicue (Great Lady Serpent Skirt) stood in the Sacred Precinct at Tenochtitlan. She was the fearsome Aztec earth-mother goddess. Coatlicue gave birth to the Aztecs' national god Huitzilopochtli, the moon goddess, and the stars.

This model (right) is based on an Aztec statue. It shows a goddess holding two children. Figures of gods were often created from moulds (left).

4 Carefully ease the little model out of the solid block, using the modelling tool. The petroleum jelly should ensure that it comes away cleanly.

5 Clean any loose bits of clay from the mould and smear petroleum jelly inside. Use a cotton-wool bud to make sure the jelly is pushed into every part.

6 Mix up some plaster of Paris and pour it into the mould. Tap the mould gently to remove any air bubbles. Leave the plaster to dry for at least an hour.

7 Gently tip the plaster statue from the mould. Dust it with a brush, then paint it a terracotta colour, so that it looks like an Aztec pottery figure.

Temples and Sacrifices

MESOAMERICAN PEOPLE believed that unless they made offerings of blood and human lives to the gods, the Sun would die and the world would come to an end. Maya rulers pricked themselves with cactus thorns and sting-ray spines, or drew spiked cords through their tongues to draw blood. They pulled out captives' fingernails so the blood flowed or threw them into holy water-holes. Aztecs pricked their ear-lobes each morning and collected two drops of blood to give to the gods. They also went to war to capture prisoners. On special occasions, vast numbers of captives were needed for sacrifice. It was reported that 20,000 victims were sacrificed to celebrate the completion of the Great Temple at Tenochtitlan in 1487. It took four days to kill them all. Mesoamerican temples were tombs as well as places of sacrifice. Rulers and their wives were buried inside. Each ruler aimed to build a great temple as a memorial to his reign.

TEMPLE TOMB
Pyramid Temple 1 at Tikal was built in the AD700s as a memorial to a Maya king. Nine stone platforms were built above the burial chamber, to create a tall pyramid shape reaching up to the sky.

HOLY KNIFE
This sacrificial knife has a blade of a semi-precious stone called chalcedony. It was made by Mixtecs from south Mexico. Mesoamerican priests used finely decorated knives of flint, obsidian and other hard stones to kill captives for sacrifice. These were trimmed to be as sharp as glass.

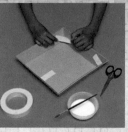

A PYRAMID TEMPLE

You will need: pencil, ruler, thick card, scissors, PVA glue, glue brush, masking tape, thin strips of balsa wood, thin card, corrugated card, water bowl, paintbrushes, paints.

Bottom level A x2 — 45 cm, 45 cm

Top level C — 21 cm

A x4 — 45 cm, 5 cm

Middle level B x2 — 33 cm, 33 cm

B x4 — 33cm, 3cm, 2cm

C x4 — 21cm, 2cm

Shrine walls — 9cm x6, 7cm, 6cm, 9cm x2, 6cm

Shrine roof x2 — 6cm, 6cm, 7cm

Cut out pieces for the pyramid and temple-top shrines from thick card, as shown above.

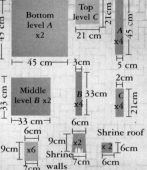

1 Use PVA glue and masking tape to join the thick card pieces to make three flat boxes (A, B and C). Leave the boxes until the glue is completely dry.

2 From the remaining pieces of card, make the two temple-top shrines, as shown. You could add extra details with strips of balsa wood or thin card.

SKULL SHRINE

Rows of human skulls, carved in stone, decorate this shrine outside the Aztecs' Great Temple in the centre of Tenochtitlan. Most Aztec temples also had skull-racks, where rows of real human heads were displayed. They were cut from the bodies of sacrificed captives.

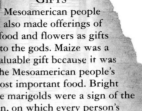

RELIGIOUS GIFTS

Mesoamerican people also made offerings of food and flowers as gifts to the gods. Maize was a valuable gift because it was the Mesoamerican people's most important food. Bright orange marigolds were a sign of the Sun, on which every person's life depended.

PERFECTION

The ideal victim for human sacrifice was a fit and healthy young man.

maize

marigolds

HUMAN SACRIFICE

This Aztec codex painting shows captives being sacrificed. At the top, you can see a priest cutting open a captive's chest and removing the heart as an offering to the gods.

This model is based on the Great Temple that stood in the centre of Tenochtitlan.

3 Glue the boxes, one on top of the next. Cut out pieces of card the same size as each side of your boxes. They should be about 1–2cm wide. Stick down, as shown.

4 Cut out two strips of card 2cm x 26cm. Glue them to a third piece of card 14cm x 26cm. Glue corrugated card 9.5cm x 26cm in position, as shown.

5 Stick the staircase to the front of the temple, as shown. Use a ruler to check that the staircase is an equal distance from either side of the temple.

7 Paint the whole temple a cream colour to look like natural stone. Add details, such as carvings or wall paintings, using brightly coloured paint.

53

Time for Celebration

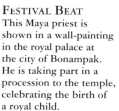

ESTIVALS, WITH MUSIC AND DANCING, were a very important part of Mesoamerican life. All big Aztec and Maya cities had a huge open space in the centre, where crowds gathered to sing and dance to honour the gods on festival days. Every twenty days, there were celebrations to mark the start of a new month. There were also festivals, with prayers and sacrifices, to mark important seasons of the farming year. In July and August, the Aztecs celebrated flowering trees and plants. In September, there were harvest festivals, and in October, festivals where hunters gave thanks for plentiful prey. For the Aztec rulers and their guests, feasts and entertainment were a regular event.

All of these special occasions involved music and song. Favourite instruments included rattles, whistles, ocarinas, flutes, bells and shells blown like trumpets. Aztec musicians also played a two-tone wooden drum, called a *teponaztli*, to provide a lively beat for dancing. Stringed instruments were unknown until after the Spanish conquest.

FESTIVAL BEAT
This Maya priest is shown in a wall-painting in the royal palace at the city of Bonampak. He is taking part in a procession to the temple, celebrating the birth of a royal child.

AN AZTEC ORCHESTRA
Musicians played conch shells, rattles and drums while crowds of worshippers sang and danced in the main square of Tenochtitlan.

AN AZTEC RATTLE

You will need: self-drying clay, modelling tool, pastry board, cling film, water bowl, dried melon seeds, bamboo cane, white and terracotta paint, paintbrush, water pot, feather, PVA glue, glue brush.

1 Make a solid model gourd from self-drying clay. You could copy the shape shown above. When it is dry, wrap the gourd completely in clingfilm.

2 Cover the wrapped model gourd with an outer layer of self-drying clay about 1cm thick. Smooth the clay with water to give an even surface.

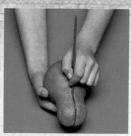

3 Leave the outer layer of clay to get hard but not completely solid. Cut it in half with the thin end of the modelling tool and remove the model gourd.

FLUTES

Wind instruments, like these Aztec flutes, were popular throughout Mesoamerica. They were used for playing tunes. Ocarinas were little round musical instruments, shaped like turtles or birds. They were blown like flutes.

MUSIC

Mesoamerican people were not skilled metalworkers, but they found plenty of other materials to make instruments from. Conch shells from the sea were cleaned to make trumpets. Rattles might be made from the shells of armadillos, from clay, or from Sun-dried gourds. Dried seeds were put inside.

gourd

melon seeds

THE RHYTHM

Drums were popular. They were often made from a hollow log and were decorated with carvings.

INSTRUMENTS

This picture from a codex shows two Aztec musicians with some of the instruments they played: a conch shell trumpet, dried-gourd rattles, and flutes made from clay. Some of the instruments are decorated with tassels and bows.

JUMPING FOR JOY

These pictures from an Aztec codex show a rattle-player, a drummer and a juggler. Acrobats, jugglers and contortionists performed at many joyful festivals, such as harvest-time celebrations.

4 Cover the edge of one half of the hollow gourd with wet clay. Put dry seeds or beans inside and a cane through the middle. Press the halves together.

5 When it is dry, decorate the rattle with painted patterns and push a feather into the top of the bamboo cane. Coat the rattle with PVA glue for a shiny finish.

Gourd-shaped rattles were very popular instruments in Mesoamerica. The seeds inside the dried gourds would provide the rattle sound. Codex pictures often show people carrying rattles in processions. The rattles were often decorated with feathers.

Sports and Games

MESOAMERICAN PEOPLE enjoyed sports and games after work and on festival days. Two favourite games were *tlachtli* or *ulama*, the famous Mesoamerican ball-game, and *patolli*, a board-game. The ball-game was played in front of huge crowds, while *patolli* was a quieter game. Mesoamerican games were not just for fun. Both the ball-game and *patolli* had religious meanings. In the first, the court symbolized the world, and the rubber ball stood for the Sun as it made its daily journey across the sky. Players were meant to keep the ball moving in order to give energy to the Sun. Losing teams were sometimes sacrificed as offerings to the Sun god. In *patolli*, the movement of counters on the board represented the passing years.

PATOLLI

A group of Aztecs are shown here playing the game of *patolli*. It was played by moving dried beans or clay counters along a cross-shaped board with 52 squares. It could be very exciting. Players often bet on the result.

THE ACROBAT

This Olmec statue shows a very supple acrobat. Mesoamericans admired youth, fitness and beauty. Sports were fun, but they could also be good training for the demands of war. Being fit was considered attractive.

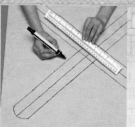

FLYING MEN

Volador was a ceremony performed on religious festival days. Four men, dressed as birds and attached to ropes, jumped off a high pole. As they spun round, falling towards the ground, they circled the pole 13 times each. That made 52 circuits – the length of the Mesoamerican holy calendar cycle.

PLAY PATOLLI

You will need: thick card, pencil, ruler, black marker pen, paints, small paintbrush, water pot, coloured papers, scissors, PVA glue and glue brush, dried broad or butter beans, self-drying clay.

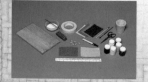

1 Measure a square of thick card about 50cm x 50cm. Using a marker pen and a ruler, draw three lines from corner to corner to make a cross-shape.

2 Draw seven pairs of spaces along each arm. The third space in from the end should be a double space. Paint triangles in it.

3 Draw eight jaguar heads and eight marigolds on differently coloured paper. Cut them out. Paint the face of the Sun god into the centre.

TARGET RING
This stone ring comes from Chichen-Itza. Ball-game players used only their hips and knees to hit a solid rubber ball through rings like this fixed high on the ball-court walls.

ALL DRESSED UP
A man dressed to play the Mesoamerican ball-game is shown in this terracotta statue. The figure was made around AD800 on the Maya island of Jaina, off the western coast of the Yucatan peninsula. He wears a protective belt of leather and wood, padded wrist-guards and knee-guards, a pointed cap and big earrings. Being a ball-game player was risky but could bring rich rewards. Winners were sometimes allowed to claim the spectators' clothes and jewels as prizes.

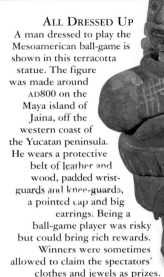

PLAY BALL
The ruins of a huge ball-court can still be seen in the Maya city of Uxmal. The biggest courts were up to 60m long and were built next to temples, in the centre of cities. People crowded inside the court to watch. Play was fast, furious and dangerous. Many players were injured as they clashed with opponents.

4 Stick the jaguars and marigolds randomly on the board. Paint a blue circle at the end of one arm, and a crown at the opposite end. Repeat in green on the other arms.

5 Paint five dried beans black with a white dot on one side. The beans will be thrown as dice. Make two counters from clay. Paint one green and one blue.

Most of the original rules for patolli have been lost. In this version, start each counter on the circle of the same colour. The aim is to move your counter to the crown of the same colour and back. Lose a turn if you land on a jaguar and get an extra turn if you land on a marigold.

Myths, Legends and Omens

THE AZTECS lived in constant fear that their world might come to an end. Ancient legends told that this had happened four times before. Each time, the world had been born again. Yet Aztec priests and astrologers did not believe that this would happen next time. If the world ended again, it would be forever. The souls of all Aztec people would be banished to a dark, gloomy underworld. The Wind of Knives would cut the flesh from their bones, and living skeletons would feast and dance with the Lord of the Dead. Then the Aztecs would vanish forever when they reached Mictlan (hell). The Maya told similar stories about the underworld – which they called Xibalba (the Place of Fright) in a great epic poem, the Popol Vuh. This poem featured two brothers, called the Hero Twins.

Aztec legends also told that the end of the world would be heralded by strange signs. In AD1519 these gloomy prophecies seemed to be coming true. Ruler Moctezuma II had weird, worrying dreams. Astronomers also observed eclipses of the Sun and a moving comet with a fiery tail.

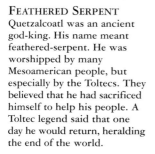

FEATHERED SERPENT
Quetzalcoatl was an ancient god-king. His name meant feathered-serpent. He was worshipped by many Mesoamerican people, but especially by the Toltecs. They believed that he had sacrificed himself to help his people. A Toltec legend said that one day he would return, heralding the end of the world.

HEROS AND LEGENDS
This ball court is in Copan, Guatemala. The ball-game featured in many Maya legends about the Hero Twins. They were skilled ball-game players and also expert hunters with deadly blow guns.

CREATURES OF LEGEND

This Maya bowl is decorated with a picture of a spider-monkey. Many different kinds of monkeys lived in the rainforests of Mesoamerica. Monkey-gods played an important part in Maya myths and legends. Because monkeys were quick and clever, the Maya believed that monkey-gods protected clever people, like scribes.

THE NEW FIRE CEREMONY

Every 52 years, the Aztecs believed that the world might come to an end. To stop this happening, they held a special ceremony. People put out their fires and stayed indoors. At sunset, priests climbed to the top of a hill and waited for the planet Venus to appear in the sky. At the moment it appeared, a captive was sacrificed to the gods. His heart was ripped out and a fire lit in his chest. The priests then sent messengers all over the Aztec lands, carrying torches to relight the fires. People then believed the world was safe for another 52 years.

HEAVENLY MESSENGER

Ruler Moctezuma is shown here observing the brilliant comet that appeared in the Mexican sky in 1519. Priests and Aztec people carefully studied the stars for messages from the gods. They remembered the old Toltec legend that said one day, the god Quetzalcoatl would return and bring the world to an end.

AZTEC HERITAGE

Many Aztec and Maya traditions still survive today. Millions of people speak Nahuatl (the Aztecs' language) or Maya languages. Aztec and Maya beliefs have mingled with Christian traditions to create new religious festivals. The most famous of these festivals is the Day of the Dead. Families bring presents of flowers and sweets shaped like skulls to their ancestors' graves.

The Coming of the Spanish

AGAINST THE AZTECS
This picture comes from *The History of the Indies*. It was written by Diego Duran, a Spanish friar who felt sympathy for the Aztecs. Spanish soldiers and their allies from Tlaxcalla are seen fighting against the Aztecs. Although the Aztecs fought bravely, they had no chance of defeating Spanish soldiers mounted on horseback and armed with guns.

IN 1493 explorer Christopher Columbus arrived back in Spain from his pioneering voyage across the Atlantic Ocean. He told tales of an extraordinary "new world" full of gold. Excited by Columbus' stories, a group of Spanish soldiers sailed to Mexico in 1519, hoping to make their fortunes. They were led by a nobleman called Hernan Cortes. Together with the Aztecs' enemies, he led a march on Tenochtitlan. For the next two years, the Aztecs fought to stop Cortes and his soldiers taking over their land. At first, they had some success, driving the Spaniards out of Tenochtitlan in May 1520. Then, in 1521, Cortes attacked the city again, set fire to its buildings and killed around three-quarters of the population. In 1535, Mexico became a colony, ruled by officials sent from Spain.

A similar thing happened in Maya lands, but more slowly. The Spanish first landed there in 1523. They did not conquer the last independent city-state, Tayasal, until 1697.

A SAD NIGHT
On 6 May 1520, Spanish soldiers massacred Aztecs gathered for a religious festival in Tenochtitlan. The citizens were outraged and attacked the Spaniards, many of whom died. During this night, the emperor Moctezuma II was stoned to death, probably by Aztecs who believed he had betrayed them. Cortes called this the *Noche Triste* (sad night).

THE END OF AZTEC POWER
This Aztec picture shows the surrender of Cuauhtemoc, the last Aztec king, to Cortes. After Moctezuma II died in 1520, the Aztecs were led by two of Moctezuma's descendants – Cuitlahuac, who ruled for only one year, and Cuauhtemoc. He was the last king and reigned until 1524.

Running for their Lives
This illustration from a Spanish manuscript shows Aztec people fleeing from Spanish conquerors. You can see heavily-laden porters carrying stocks of food and household goods across a river to safety. On the far bank, mothers and children, with a pet bird and dog, hide behind huge maguey cactus plants.

Working like Slaves
Spanish settlers in Mexico took over all the Aztec and Maya fields and forced the people to work as farm labourers. They treated them cruelly, almost like slaves. This modern picture shows a Spanish overseer giving orders.

After the Conquest
Mexican artist Diego Rivera shows Mesoamerica after the Spanish conquest. Throughout the 1500s and 1600s, settlers from Spain arrived there. They drove out the local nobles and forced ordinary people to work for them. Spanish missionaries tried to replace local beliefs with European customs and Christianity. In Tenochtitlan, the Spaniards pulled down splendid Aztec palaces and temples to build churches and fine homes for themselves. You can see gangs of Aztec men working as labourers in the background of this picture.

Glossary

A

adobe Sun-dried mud bricks, used as a building material.

ahaw One of the special names the Maya gave to their rulers.

amaranth A bushy plant with edible seeds.

amate Paper made from fig tree bark.

ancestor A family member who died long ago.

atlatl A spear-thrower, made of wood. It acted as an extension of the arm, so that the spears could be thrown with greater force.

Aztecs Mesoamerican people who lived in northern and central Mexico. They were at their most powerful between AD1350 and AD1520.

B

ball-court The place where the Mesoamerican ball-game was played. A large, open courtyard surrounded by rows of stone seats.

barter Exchanging goods for others of equal value.

C

calpulli An Aztec family or neighbourhood group. The *calpulli* enforced law and order. It also arranged education, training and welfare benefits for its members.

causeway A roadway raised above the surrounding land or water.

cenote A holy waterhole, or natural well occurring in limestone areas. Here captives or other valuable possessions were sacrificed as offerings to the gods.

Chacmool A stone statue in the shape of a dying warrior or a rain god, carrying a dish in his arms. The dish was used to hold blood or hearts from human sacrifices. Chacmool statues have been found in many Mesoamerican lands.

chalcedony A reddish semi-precious stone.

chia A bushy plant with edible seeds.

chinampa An Aztec garden built on the fertile, reclaimed land on the lake shore.

chultun An underground tank for storing water.

cihuacoatl The Aztecs' name for their deputy leader.

clan A group of people related to one another through their ancestors or by marriage.

cochineal A red dye made from crushed beetles.

codex A folding book.

compost Rotting vegetation used to make the soil fertile.

conch-shell The huge horn-shaped shell of a tropical sea creature. It was used as a musical instrument in Mesoamerican lands.

D

dugout canoe A type of canoe made by hollowing out a tree trunk.

G

garrison A band of soldiers living in a particular place.

glyph A picture-symbol used in the Mesoamerican system of writing.

H

herbalism Trying to heal people by using medicines made of herbs.

Huastecs Mesoamerican people who lived in coastal west Mexico. They were most powerful between around AD500 and AD1400.

huautli A bush with edible seeds.

human sacrifice Killing humans as an offering to the gods.

I

inscribed Letters or pictures carved on stone or another hard material.

J

jade A smooth, green stone. Jade was highly prized in Mesoamerica.

K

katun A Maya measurement of time – 72,000 days.

L

litter A portable bed on which Mesoamerican rulers were carried.
loom A piece of equipment used to weave cloth.

M

macehualli The Aztec name for ordinary people.
makina One of the special names the Maya gave to their rulers.
maquahuitl An Aztec war-club.
Maya Mesoamerican people who lived in southern Mexico and Guatemala. They were at their most powerful between AD250 and AD900. Their civilization went on after their lands were invaded by the Spanish in AD1527.
Mixtecs Mesoamerican people who lived in southern Mexico. They were at their most powerful between AD1300 and AD1500.
mosaic Tiny pieces of stone, shell or glass used to decorate objects.

O

obsidian A black, glassy stone. It is produced when volcanoes erupt.
ocarina A musical instrument played by blowing into it.
overseer A superviser or boss.
Olmecs A Mesoamerican people who lived in southern central Mexico. They were at their most powerful between 1200BC and 400BC.

P

patolli A popular Aztec boardgame for two players.
peccary A wild pig.
peninsula An area of land surrounded by sea on three sides, making it almost like an island.
plaza A big open space in the centre of a town or city.
pochteca Aztec merchants.
pulque An Aztec beer.

Q

quetzal A rainforest bird with beautiful, long, green tail-feathers.

R

rock-crystal A transparent, semi-precious stone.

S

silt Fine grains of soil found at the bottom of rivers and lakes.
slash and burn A method of farming in the rainforest.
slip Clay mixed with water and minerals to form a liquid. It was used to decorate pottery.
stele A tall stone pillar.
sting-ray A fish with a long, poisonous spike in its tail.
stucco Plaster used to cover and decorate important stone buildings, such as temples.

T

tamales Dumplings made of maize with a meat or vegetable filling.
terracotta Baked clay.
tlachtli The Aztec name for the ball-game played throughout Mesoamerica.
tlatoani The Aztec name for their ruler.
Toltecs Mesoamerican people who lived in and around Tula, a city in central Mexico. They were at their most powerful around AD950 to AD1150.
tortillas Maize pancakes.
tribute Taxes paid in goods by conquered people.
tumpline A band of cloth, worn over the shoulders. The tumpline helped porters carry heavy loads.
turquoise A beautiful blue-green semi-precious stone.

U

uictli A Mesoamerican digging stick used like a spade.

V

volador An Aztec religious ritual in which four men spun round and round a tall pole.

Y

yucca A desert plant with long, fleshy leaves.

Index